COMMUNICATING
WITH IMPACT

Communicating With IMPACT ™
Copyright © 2017, Patrick Donadio
www.patrickdonadio.com

Published by:
Peffer Press
Columbus, Ohio

Hardcover: 978-1-944160-00-5
Paperback: 978-1-944160-01-2
eBook: 978-1-944160-02-9

First Edition

Printed in the United States of America

COMMUNICATING
WITH IMPACT

A Guide to Leadership Communication:

Effectively Communicate Ideas and Achieve Greater Results

A powerful six-step process for presentation and speaking skills, media training, and tools for interpersonal communications.

PATRICK DONADIO

Peffer Press
Columbus, Ohio 2017

Praise for *Communicating with IMPACT*

"*Communicating with IMPACT* shows you a simple method for designing powerful communication but goes way beyond the basics. It provides tactics and techniques that most leaders never consider or use that will make you far more effective in your spoken and written messages. Apply this process and increase the impact of your communication."

— Mark Sanborn, President of Sanborn & Associates, Inc., New York Times and Wall Street Journal Best-Selling Author of several books including *The Fred Factor, Fred 2.0*, and *You Don't Need a Title to Be a Leader*

"Patrick Donadio is a masterful communication coach and he has helped my team prepare to communicate their results for our successful National Institute of Health (NIH) accreditation process. In *Communicating with IMPACT*, Donadio reveals his proven, practical process that you too can use to create the results you desire whether in front of a group or interpersonally."

— Michael A. Caligiuri, MD, Healthcare Executive

"Because good communication skills are vital to building relationships in our personal and professional lives, you'll want to buy *Communicating with IMPACT*...immediately. Patrick has written a book that is useful to anyone who appreciates a practical, easy-to-read book that will teach you a proven process to construct your message, engage your receiver, and inspire others to action."

— Susan RoAne, Best-Selling Author of *How to Work a Room*

"If you want a quick fix, *Communicating with IMPACT* is not for you. If you want transformation, have the guts to look a little deeper. Leadership is about communicating a vision, and visions come from what is best and deepest inside of us. The magic of IMPACT is that it is a process of reflection and discovery that gives clarity to that vision."

— Tim Ryan, U.S. Congressman and Author of *A Mindful Nation*

"You need a message with impact to get noticed in the world today. Patrick Donadio delivers a knockout punch."

— Jeffrey Hayzlett, Primetime TV & Podcast Host, Chairman of C-Suite Network, Best-Selling Author

"*Communicating with IMPACT* is easy to understand and implement. I have used Patrick many times to teach/coach our professionals how to communicate technical matters in terminology our clients understand and appreciate. Read this book and become a master at listening louder and speaking with a focused intention. No matter your age, position at work, or walk of life, this book will transform your way of thinking and behaviors in communicating with others."

— Charles R. Ciuni, Partner at Deloitte LLP

"*Communicating with IMPACT* provides a great model to use in crafting any communication, from asking your boss for a raise to inspiring thousands to act. The book is also full of rules, tools, and exercises to fine-tune each step. I will keep a copy on my desk to make sure I say things right the first time!"

— Marcia Reynolds, PsyD, global Expert on Workplace Communications and Author of *The Discomfort Zone: How Leaders Turn Difficult Conversations Into Breakthroughs*

"Far too many sales are lost due to the salesperson's inability to communicate effectively with the customer. Customers speak one language, while salespeople speak a different one. Ultimately, nobody is truly listening. Patrick's book is the definitive 'playbook' every salesperson should read to improve their selling skills. He doesn't just give you new tools; he clearly outlines how you can execute them to their fullest. You will definitely see a return on your investment with this book!"

— Mark Hunter, Author of *High Profit Selling: Win the Sale Without Compromising On Price*

"In a world where so many people mistakenly think they've communicated after they speak, or write a memo, or send out a tweet, it's refreshing to hear Patrick Donadio remind us that communicating is a two-way connection between people. In this book, he maps out a clear and practical plan that can help anyone make those connections with impact."

— Will Kopp, Chief Communications Officer, Ohio Wesleyan University

Foreword

Humanity today forms a global tribe. Those without the communication skills that create a meaningful impact will find themselves outside the circle of significance. Those who learn to communicate with impact with people at all levels and from a variety of cultures and backgrounds will be the pacesetters of the coming generations.

I came to the United States as a teenager with little knowledge of English and only fifty dollars in my pocket. I knew that if I wanted to achieve success and significance in business and in life, I would need to master the art of effective communication. Since 2005, I've had the honor of interacting each day with thousands of students, faculty, and staff at High Point University, and I continue to see how communication is not only about words; it's about creating a personal connection. When something becomes personal, it becomes important. That is the essence of effective communication. It's not so much that we need to communicate; it's that we need to connect: to create a personal connection with clients, associates, friends, and family.

In *Communicating with IMPACT*, Patrick lays out the comprehensive approach to communicating, speaking, and connecting that he has used to work with students and startups, as well as with Fortune 500 company leaders and CEOs. The simple yet powerful method he presents is deeply rooted in his long and successful career as a professional speaker, a masterful coach, an effective consultant, and a respected business leader. In fact, he is one of only four people in the world to hold both the Certified Speaking Professional (CSP) and Master Certified Coach (MCC) designations.

I have known Patrick Donadio for over twenty years. We first met at the National Speakers Association, where we both are members. Over the years, I have seen how Patrick's involvement, serving as committee chairs and now on the national board, allows him to mentor new speakers in the same way that he mentors C-Suite leaders, with humility and enthusiasm. That same spirit is in this book, and in his IMPACT approach to communication.

Donadio's easy-to-learn and hard-to-master system can improve the bottom line of any business, and significantly impact the potential for success of anyone. Patrick teaches about making an impact, not simply talking. He takes the reader through the complicated maze of relationships, and his proprietary IMPACT process is the map that is easy to read and follow.

There can be no better guide down the path towards communicating with IMPACT than Patrick Donadio. Enjoy this journey; it will bring you far.

Dr. Nido R. Qubein,
President, High Point University;
Chairman, Great Harvest Bread Company

Table of Contents

INTRODUCTION
Communicating with IMPACT

In an environment of constant technological change, we communicate in countless ways. But how effective are we in our communication?

We spend as much as 80 percent of our waking day in some form of communication.

Whether speaking with our co-workers, making a presentation to a potential client, doing a media interview about a new product, leaving a voicemail message for a client, sending an email to our boss, messaging through various forms of software, texting a colleague, tweeting, posting a Facebook status, or anything else, we are trying to communicate something to someone in order to achieve an outcome and make an impact.

However, many times the communication fails and we don't get the outcome we intended. Have you ever experienced a message that was misinterpreted, a conversation that didn't produce the results intended, or an interaction that was a waste of time? If so, usually one's first (and incorrect) inclination is to blame the other person for this. One thing I learned over my many years as a consultant, educator, leader, coach, teacher, speaker, client, parent, husband, and human being, is that the true meaning of the message comes from the receiver, not necessarily the sender. Moreover, if this is the case, then I (the sender) am just as much (or more) to blame for any confusion as the receiver.

2

My hope is that this book will help you craft and deliver a focused and concise message that is clearly understood by the receiver – a message that achieves its intended result.

Over the past three decades, I have worked at both ends of the spectrum, with Executives/CEOs in corporate America and college graduates who are trying to get their first job. They all had similar challenges. How do you get your message across and communicate with impact?

As you read this book, I have the following three goals for you to aim towards and eventually accomplish:

1. **Build on your strengths.** I want to remind you of the things you know, that you are already doing, in order to help you be more confident and be able to identify your strengths. The better you feel about yourself, the better you will perform, and the greater your impact on others will be. If it works, do more of it!

2. **Use what you know.** It's not what you know; it's what you do with what you know. As you read this book, you will be reminded of the things you know, and are not currently doing. This will help you identify things you should start doing in order to improve and be a better communicator.

3. **Change the way you impact others forever.** The Communicating with IMPACT process is made up of six principles you can easily employ to improve the way you communicate with others in just about any situation.

The IMPACT Process, when applied, will help you improve your communication skills by inspiring action, deepening your relationships, and as a consequence, helping you to achieve extraordinary results in less time.

Why Develop Your Communication Skills

Better communication leads to better results. Learning to be a better communicator can have a huge impact on you and your organization. Here are a few reasons why you might want read this book and improve your communication skills:

1. Communication Skills

A recent study from job market research firm Burning Glass Technologies[1] analyzed 25 million online job postings from more than 40,000 sources and identified the most sought-after skills. Communication skills ranked as the most or second-most desired baseline skill in all industries.

"We tend to focus on technical skill requirements, but the reality is employers are very vocal about the need for people to have foundational or baseline skills," said Matt Sigelman, CEO of Burning Glass Technologies. "Even in jobs that are really denominated in technical terms, it's still very important to employers that people have the right soft skills."

Across all jobs, an average of 1 in every 3 skills requested in a posting is a baseline skill. And in jobs generally associated with specific technical skills, such as in the healthcare and information technology fields, 1 in 4 skills listed by employers are soft skills.

2. Grooming Future Leaders

In an online poll conducted by the American Society for Training and Development (ASTD)[2], 96 percent of 369 respondents said there was a skills gap in their organizations, or that they expected one within the next year. When asked to identify the skills gaps their organizations are experiencing today, the respondents ranked these as the three most important:

55.46% managerial/supervisory skills

50.14% communication/interpersonal skills

45.10% leadership/executive-level skills

Communication and interpersonal skills play a vital role in being an effective leader. They transcend all levels of leadership. Are you and/or your organization experiencing any skills gaps in these three areas above?

Effective communication skills are critical to an organization's success. Yet many organizations' leaders and potential leaders are not being groomed, trained, or coached on how to be a more skillful communicator.

---

1   *"The Human Factor: The Hard Time Employers Have Finding Soft Skills," a new study of job postings by Burning Glass Technologies. November 2015 http://burning-glass.com/wp-content/uploads/Human_Factor_Baseline_Skills_FINAL.pdf*

2   *American Society for Training & Development, "Bridging the Skills Gap," 2006 ASTD Press. Available from www.astd.org.*

3. Increase Performance

Better communication also leads to an increase in people's performance. According to recent research by Bersin & Associates[3], companies that excel at employee recognition are twelve times more likely to generate strong business results than those that do not. They also found that in companies where recognition occurs, employee engagement, productivity, and customer service are about 14% better than in those that rarely use recognition.

In addition to recognition, most experts agree that we need the following additional skills to sustained high performance in the knowledge economy:

- **Adaptability:** The capacity to change in response to ever-shifting conditions in the economy and the marketplace, and to master the new skills that such changes require quickly.

- **Innovative thinking and action:** The ability to think creatively and to generate new ideas and solutions to challenges at work.

- **Personal responsibility for learning:** The willingness of individuals to take responsibility for continually improving their work-related capabilities throughout their careers.

In order to compete in today's global environment, individuals and organizations must increase their performance levels. This will lead to increased profits.

4. Increase Profits

For years I have been telling my clients that better communication leads to better results. A study published by Watson Wyatt Worldwide[4] confirms my point. When they surveyed 328 companies from around the world with five million combined workers, they found that companies that communicate more effectively, especially during trying economic times, are more effective in achieving their desired results.

According to the report, the financial results of good communication are also substantial. They found that companies with effective communication had 47 % higher returns to shareholders over five years.

---

3   *http://www.bersin.com/News/Content.aspx?id=16023*

4   *Watson Wyatt Worldwide, "Capitalizing on Effective Communication", 2009-2010. Available from www.towerswatson.com. Last accessed Dec. 2015.*

"Forget supply and demand. Forget computers. Today, communication, not computation, drives change. We are rushing into a world where connectivity is everything and where old business know-how means nothing."

— *Kevin Kelly*

5. Deeper Relationships

Let's go back to the basics. Our number one resource is our people.

For people to perform better, they have to learn how to communicate better. We build our relationships over time, in multiple interactions with others. By communicating with impact, it will become simpler for them to connect with others and achieve a more powerful result.

We can all impact others in many ways, just as an object impacts another object. Imagine a meteor hitting the earth. You have a surface impact that changes the surface of one object while the core of the object stays the same. If the meteor hits the ocean, the surface might return to its original state quickly. Or the same meteor could have a deep impact, one that not only affects the surface, but also penetrates through the surface and into the core of the other object. Both the surface and the core are affected. Now imagine that in terms of our message to someone else.

When communicating with impact, the message transforms the outside of your receiver, however a deep impact transforms part of their core: who they are, how they think, and what they believe. A deep impact transforms what they do and helps them change their behavior in order to achieve the desired result.

The goal of every communication or interaction doesn't have to be making a deep impact. In many cases, a surface impact is an accomplishment (just getting people to do something different).

As a coach, I often experience deep impact with my clients, and when it happens, it can be very rewarding. In order for this to happen it usually takes a series of interactions over a period of time with a process I call "layered learning." This is where you learn new skills or shift beliefs by building on what you learned from each previous session in order to help the individual learn and grow.

Nevertheless, deeper relationships lead to trust, trust leads to change, and change leads to results.

"Communication is a two way street, I talk, you listen...."

— *A Linear Communicator*

End the Culture of Linear Communication

More and more senders are opting for written communication over verbal, even when the receiver is right down the hall or across the room. This not only changes the nature of the work environment, making it less relational, it also adds to confusion and miscommunication.

The reason for this is that written communication is a form of linear communication, which is what happens when you have a Sender who sends a message without any feedback from the Receiver. Here is what it looks like:

This mode of communication is also referred to as one-way communication, downward communication, parent-to-child communication, autocratic communication, and so on.

What it boils down to is this: because there is no feedback in linear communication, your message may not be the same one actually received.

The solution is two-way communication, where the Receiver sends feedback to the Sender:

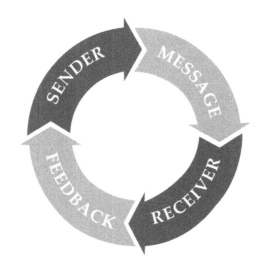

In my Communicating with IMPACT workshops, we do a brief exercise to demonstrate linear communication in action. I first ask audience attendees to find a partner so they can test their communication skills.

I ask one person in the two-person team to act as the Sender and remain facing a screen where I will show an image for the exercise.

The other person plays the role of the Receiver and I ask them to turn their chair around, so they cannot see the screen, and to grab a pen and a piece of paper and get ready to draw.

I tell the Sender, "Your job is to describe this picture on the screen to the best of your ability to the Receiver so your partner can draw this picture." I remind the Sender, "Remember, this is linear communication, so there is no talking and you are not allowed to look at the person or their paper because this would be a form of feedback."

Next, I remind the Receiver (who is facing away from the screen) that this is one-way communication and they are not allowed ask any questions or turn around at any time to look at the screen.

To make this more realistic, just like in the workplace, I give them a time limit. Every day we have deadlines and have to be able to communicate information in a short amount of time. I set my timer to one minute and yell, "Go!"

During this time, the noise level in the room increases as all the Senders try to describe the picture to the Receivers. As I walk around the room, I notice Senders struggling as they try to describe the geometric figure on the screen to their partner while they are not allowed to get any feedback from them. Occasionally, I catch a few Senders trying to glance at the Receiver's paper. I give the group a 20-second warning and you can hear the noise level increase as people frantically try to finish the exercise.

As the timer finally goes off, the Senders start looking at the drawings and you can see them all smiling and laughing. They want to see how well they did at describing the picture and what they see is nothing like the picture on the screen. We have a good time with this. I have done this exercise for over twenty years and very rarely do more than one or two people in the group draw a picture that matches up.

The point is clear—linear communication, where no feedback is available, is not the most effective form of communication. Linear communication may work well for the communication of a simple message. However the more important or complicated the message, the less likely linear communication will be the best approach.

Linear communication plays out every day in the working world, not just when we send an email, text message, or even write a letter. It also happens verbally in our fast-paced world when managers quickly give directions to employees, employees speedily give information to customers, or in our personal life, when a parent tells a child what to do. In each case it is done quickly with the assumption that the Receiver understands, with no apparent need for clarification.

The Communicating with IMPACT process can work very well for improving linear communication. However, in this book I chose to focus more on face-to-face conversations and speaking or presenting to groups or the media.

The Communication with IMPACT Process

The Communicating with IMPACT Process is made up of two sections:

The Planning phase (IMP)

The Action phase (ACT)

Planning Phase (IMP)

The three components of the Planning Phase (IMP) help you formulate your ideas, craft your message, and identify the Receiver of your message. You could also call this phase the "I M Planning to ACT" phase – as in I am planning to act.

I – Intention

Why communicate? The planning phase starts with the "why" behind the message. Start by asking yourself a few questions:

Why am I communicating with this person?

What is the intended outcome of this communication, both for me and for the receiver?

As a result of this communication, what do I want the other person to think, do, or feel?

The clearer you understand and develop your intention, the clearer your message will be.

M – Message

What is the Message? The message is what we say, write, or otherwise communicate both verbally and non-verbally. This message helps us to achieve our intention.

We should carefully craft our message and choose the appropriate method of delivery so that we can have the desired impact on the receiver.

P – Person

Who is the Receiver? How do you personalize your Message to this receiver?

We all learned the Golden Rule in elementary school: "Do unto others as you would have them do unto you." In other words, treat people the way that you want to be treated. What your teachers did not tell you in elementary school is that not everyone has the same personality or communication preferences.

When it comes to communicating in our complicated modern world, I would much prefer you practice what Dr. Tony Alessandra calls his Platinum Rule®. "Treat others the way they want to be treated," or "Do unto others as they want done unto them."

You do this with a simple three-step process:

1. As the Sender, identify your communication behavior style.
2. Indentify the communication style and preferences of your Receiver.
3. Blend the styles of the Sender and Receiver in order to enhance the communication and to increase the impact of your message.

Action Phase (ACT)

The three components of the Action Phase (ACT) will help you communicate your message so that it achieves the Intention you set at the beginning. This phase also seeks to increase the impact of the message in order to achieve a better result.

A – Activate

How do you engage your Receiver in communication?

Most people have shorter attention spans these days and, in order to keep their attention, you will need to activate the Receiver and engage the Receiver physically, mentally, and emotionally.

C – Clarify

How do you make sure the message that you sent is the same message that has been received?

Many times your message may not be received or interpreted the way you want it to be.

Clarify throughout your communication in order to make sure the message you send is the same one received, and in turn, make sure the message they send back to you is the same one you receive.

T – Transform

How do you transform your message into results so that you can achieve your intention?

If you communicate and nothing changes, then you are not communicating with impact.

Here are a few ways to check and see if the transformation occurred:

Was there any movement (physically, mentally, and/or emotionally) as a result of this communication?

Are you closer to achieving your original intention as a result of this communication?

Did you identify the next steps you and the receiver must take in order to make the intention a reality?

When do these steps need to take place?

What follow-up communication needs to occur? By whom? By when?

Even though Transform is the sixth and last principle of the Communicating with IMPACT process, transformation occurs throughout, not only at the end. Active transformation is initiated in this principle, but emotional and intellectual transformation has to begin much earlier in the process.

> *"The greatest sign of a successful person is one who takes action to make it happen. Words are often lost in translation."*
>
> — *Michael Jordan*

IMPACT Quiz

These are some of the questions I ask my coaching clients to help them identify areas to improve their communication skills. How do you rate?

(Circle "yes," "no," or "maybe")

1. Do you have a clear idea of your intention for your communication before you start?

　　　Yes　　No　　Maybe

2. Do you use a communication process to plan your message?

　　　Yes　　No　　Maybe

3. Do you adapt your message to the communication personality style of your receiver?

　　　Yes　　No　　Maybe

4. Are you comfortable speaking to groups or the media?

　　　Yes　　No　　Maybe

5. Do you actively engage your receiver physically, mentally, and/or emotionally?

　　　Yes　　No　　Maybe

6. Do you use techniques to clarify misunderstandings to check and see if the message you send is the same one received?

　　　Yes　　No　　Maybe

7. Do you help the receiver transform your message into results?

　　　Yes　　No　　Maybe

Note: Look at the questions to which you answered "No." These may be some areas you might want to focus on in this book.

(To download more IMPACT resources , go to http://www.PatrickDonadio.com)

How to Use This Book?

As you go through the book, each chapter is geared toward teaching you one of the six principles to be more effective in communicating with IMPACT.

Once you finished the book, you can use it in one of two ways. Either you can use the complete process from start to finish, or use the book in bits and pieces as needed. Here are a few tips for either approach:

IMPACT – From Start to Finish

When you face a very challenging communication, you will want to walk through all the principles of the IMPACT process in order to plan, structure, and deliver your message.

What if you need to have a difficult conversation with an employee about a behavior issue and you have been putting it off because you don't know what to say? This is the perfect time to walk through the six principles and craft the conversation before you have it.

Or, you are preparing for an important presentation to the board and are feeling nervous about delivering your message. Using the Communicating with IMPACT process will not only help you plan and structure your presentation, but in the act of planning, it will help you feel more comfortable and confident.

Or, you just received a call from the communication department informing you that tomorrow they want you to talk to the local newspaper reporter about the role your company is playing in the United Way Campaign. Walking through the IMPACT process will be a great tool to help you prepare for this media interview.

As you can see, there are many occasions where using the IMPACT process from start to finish will be a valuable tool you can use to be a better communicator.

However, there will also be times when you just need a little help and will want to look at only one or two of the principles in the process.

IMPACT – Piece by Piece

This book was designed to be a practical guide. Once you have finished reading it, I suggest you keep it on your desk or close by so you can reach for it whenever you feel stuck, uncomfortable, or confused as you are crafting a message (e-mail, text, or letter) or preparing for a conversation with someone.

You may be better at some principles than others so remind yourself which principles are ones that you need focus on. Feel free to write in this book, put Post It® Flags on certain pages, or use a highlighter to underline key sections. This is a resource guide for you so do whatever it takes to make this book helpful for your everyday communication.

Let's say you are preparing for a presentation and you are concerned that you might be doing too much talking and not engaging the audience enough? You could flip over to the Activate chapter and get a few pointers on how to activate the audience.

You are having an important second meeting with a prospective client and you want to try to identify their communication style so you can prepare for the meeting. You can turn to the People chapter and see what style they are and how you can adjust your communication style to build a better relationship.

On the other hand, if you have an important meeting with one of your team members and you know that you really have to get some tasks done and done quickly, you could turn to the Transform chapter and see how you might structure the conversation to make sure things get done.

You get the idea.

> "If both of you haven't received the same message, then you
> haven't communicated."

IMPACT Insight: How well have you communicated?

In order to gain a better understanding of how well you have communicated with someone, try asking yourself the next three questions following your communication:

1. "Is the message that I was sending the same message they received?"

2. "Has there been any change as a result of this communication?"

3. "Am I closer to achieving the intention I set for this interaction?"

If you answered "yes" to all of these, great! If not, don't be too worried – even master communicators sometimes fail to successfully achieve their intended results. That is what this book is intended to help you with, so just keep reading!

The Communicating with IMPACT process is tried and true. It has worked for my clients and me over the past 20 years and it will work for you once you put it into practice.

Here is my challenge for you: after you read each principle, go out and use that specific principle right away. That way, you will immediately start achieving remarkable results with this process. Please feel free to e-mail me your results so we can learn from each other.

Keep Communicating with IMPACT!

Patrick Donadio

patrick@patrickdonadio.com

PHASE 1
THE PLANNING PHASE

I	Intention
M	Message
P	Person

Intention (ĭn-tĕn'shən) – noun

an aim that guides action; an objective; a purpose; a design

a determination to act in a certain way: resolve

Principle 1

INTENTION

- Crafting a Laser-Focused Intention (LFI)
- Laser-Focused Intention (LFI) Template
- LFI is Like a GPS
- What's Your Intention? (Checklist)
- Intention Tool: Employ Outcome Thinking
- Different Intentions for Different Roles
- Secondary Intentions (SI)
- Align Your Communication to Your Mission
- IMPACT Insight
- IMPACT Reflection
- IMPACT Application

INTENTION

MESSAGE

PERSON

ACTIVATE

CLARIFY

TRANSFORM

Principle 1

INTENTION

"If you don't know where you are going, you will probably end up someplace else."

— *Dr. David Campbell*

I is for INTENTION

Why communicate? The planning phase starts with the "why" behind the message.

The first principle in the IMPACT process is the intention. An intention is an aim that guides your communication or action, an objective, purpose, or outcome. It is the "why" behind the message.

Before you start your communication, spend a few moments to identify your intention by asking yourself a few questions:

- Why am I communicating with this person?

- What is my intent/outcome for this communication?

- What is their intention for this communication?

- As a result of the communication, what do we want the other person to think, do, or feel?

What it comes down to is this: the clearer your intention is, the clearer your message will be.

Did you ever feel like a conversation was heading in the wrong direction?

A few years ago, my father-in-law, Frank Kennard, told me a story about how one CEO reset the intention for a conversation in a unique and powerfully effective way.

Frank (whom I call Dad) spent much of his career interacting with company leaders in his role as a Commercial Bank Vice President. One afternoon Dad was meeting with the CEO and CFO of a large Midwestern retail chain with almost two thousand retail outlets.

Sitting at the conference table, Dad faced the glass windows overlooking the corridor to the office, and through the venetian blinds, he could see someone walking very briskly towards them. It appeared to be an office employee. Soon he heard a loud knock on the door. The CEO said, "Come in."

A young man rushed in with a very concerned look on his face. He said in a frustrated tone, "Mr. CEO, we have a problem."

The CEO seemed very intrigued by this comment. You could see him lean forward as his eyes widened. He paused for a moment and then slowly stood up. Looking directly in his employee's eyes, he calmly responded, "Young man, at this company we don't have problems. We only have opportunities."

What the CEO did next amazed my father-in-law.

He slowly raised his hand, pointed to the door, and said, "Now please go out, come back in, and let's start this conversation over."

Dad could not believe what he had just heard. It seemed almost like they were in the process of shooting a movie and the director wanted that actor to redo the scene to make it better, so he yelled, "Cut."

The young financial officer had left the office, closed the door behind him, waited a moment, and then knocked again. The CEO again said, "Come in."

The employee walked back in and said confidently, "Mr. CEO, we have an opportunity."

My father-in-law was very impressed with how the CEO had reset the tone of the conversation. The CEO understood that the intention of the conversation was what would drive the result.

Crafting a Laser-Focused Intention (LFI)

The young employee had told his CEO, "We have a problem." In other words, he had come into the office with a Problem-Focused Intention (PFI). The CEO understood that this negative PFI could drive the conversation. So the CEO reset the intention of the conversation by stating: "We only have opportunities."

By doing so, he shifted the focus to a positive, solution-focused intention. This is the beginnings of crafting your Laser-Focused Intention (LFI).

Below is my method for creating a clear, Laser-Focused Intention (LFI).

Laser-Focused Intention (LFI) Template

(To download this template, go to http://bit.ly/lfimodel)

1. "I am going to communicate with_____

                                            (Person)

2. ... about _____

                    (Message)

3. ... so that they will _____

              (Intention - Think/Do/Feel)

4. ... by a deadline of _____

                (Transform)

Notice the LFI includes four of the six principles of the IMPACT Process — Person, Message, Intention, and Transform.

Once you have completed the LFI template, you can begin to determine the intention of your communication. A good LFI starts with gathering facts and information. Like a doctor, your first goal is to diagnose before you prescribe. You want to take into account what you are trying to accomplish by having this communication: What are you trying to achieve and accomplish through this communication? What is the main concern or issue?

In my business development workshops, I tell my attendees that their real title is not what is written on their business card. Their real title should be Solution Provider. Whether a leader, salesperson, manager, presenter, consultant, physician, lawyer, accountant, spouse, parent, or friend, everyone is in the business of providing solutions.

Intention Tool: 30 Second Rule

If I only had 30 seconds, what would I want my Receiver to think, do, and/ or feel?

LFI is Like a GPS

Your intention is like your own internal Global Positioning System (GPS). It helps you stay focused on the outcome or destination of your communication.

In order to firm up your GPS-like intention, think about bridging the gap between where you are now and where you want to be, as a result of this communication.

Answer the following three questions about your communication to get started:

1. Where are you now?

2. Where do you want to be?

3. How do you get from here to there?

Plan your communication using your GPS intention: the answers to the three questions above.

There are many different intentions for communicating. Below are a few examples. Check off ones that you tend to use most often. Pay attention to the ones you do not use. Should you be using them? When would they be beneficial?

What is your intention?

Here is a list of intentions. Which ones do you use most often? Which ones would you like to start using?

Inform	Recognize	Debate
Discover	Correct	Encourage
Build Rapport	Investigate	Translate
Coach	Delegate	Negotiate
Counsel	Dominate	Laugh
Persuade	Deliver	Command
Motivate	Connect	Demand
Manage	Accelerate	Care
Mentor	Ascertain	Other examples:
Discipline	Empower	_____
Think	Explain	_____

INTENTION

MESSAGE

PERSON

ACTIVATE

CLARIFY

TRANSFORM

Ending Up Somewhere Else

Have you been to a meeting that lasted more than two hours and wondered, Why am I here? At that meeting, we both know that the person speaking and/or in charge of organizing it was not clear on their intention.

Have you ever begun a conversation where you started to talk with somebody and all of a sudden you realized you didn't know what you were talking about? Or that conversation lasted longer than you had intended? It is more likely that you did not have a clear intention in mind before you started.

Once, I had a client call me and say that they wanted me to come to their office because they wanted to pick my brain for some ideas. Because I am a coach and a consultant, it is not unusual for people to call and ask for my ideas or input. So I agreed, and then I traveled to his office and we had a conversation. I use the word conversation loosely here, because for the next hour, the client started talking, and then kept talking and talking and talking, and never asked for any of my input.

As the saying goes, the customer is always right. So I did not complain, as I realized the client's intention was simply for me to be a sounding board that day, not a coach. However, that is not what my client communicated to me. He had told me that his intention was to have me come over and share some of my ideas. The intention was unclear, and our interaction was not as fruitful as it might otherwise have been.

Intention Tool: Employ "Outcome Thinking"

When planning a communication, instead of starting at the beginning, start at the end of the conversation. Answer this question first:

• What do you want to have happen as a result of this communication?

Be clear as to what your intention is. This is where the LFI model comes in handy.

Now, still focused on the end (LFI), ask yourself, what did I say or do to make this happen? List all the ideas that you think had to happen to take you from where you are now - the present to where you want to be - to this end. Basically, you are breaking down the communication and then reconstructing it before you communicate it.

Think strategically as you prepare to communicate. Rehearse the conversation in your mind and try to anticipate his/her response. Then make the necessary adjustments before you have the real conversation.

Different Intentions for Different Roles

Let's look at how different intentions might impact an interaction. If I was meeting with a client and my intention was to mentor him or her, I might interact differently than if my intention was to manage or coach him or her. The intention drives the interaction.

As a leader and entrepreneur for the past thirty years, I have played a variety of roles with people. Here are a few examples of the various roles and services I have performed and my interpretation of the intention for each role:

• Consultants

As a consultant to organizations, I am an outside expert coming in with the intention of both identifying problems and providing solutions for the organization's challenges. People hire consultants to solve their problems.

• Mentors

As both a speaker and coach, I have mentored other current or potential speakers and coaches. Mentors have knowledge and wisdom about certain situations and surroundings because they have already experienced them. Mentors work with others with the intention to teach and guide someone else through similar professional situations and surroundings.

• Managers

I served in various managerial roles prior to starting my own business. A manager's intention is to tell his or her charged employees what they should do and how they should do it. This is quite different from the role and intention of a coach.

• Coaches

When I started professional coaching in the mid 1990s, many people did not understand the role or intention of a coach. A coach's intention is to help a client explore an issue or challenge by assisting them in uncovering the answers for themselves.

Unlike a manager, instead of giving people the answers, a true coach uses questions to help people solve their own problem or challenge.

These are my interpretations of the intentions for each role in my own career. However, things are not always cut and dry. There have been times when I have played a variety of roles with the same client. For example, I sometimes play a consultative coaching role when I am coaching on a specific skill like presentation skills. As a consultative coach, I will not only ask my client to come up with the answers but will also teach some skills to

INTENTION

MESSAGE

PERSON

ACTIVATE

CLARIFY

TRANSFORM

help them be a better presenter.

As you can see, the LFI intention you possess about the role you are playing will impact the LFI intention you have for your communication while playing that role. When playing a coach role, my intention will be to get the other person talking, versus when playing a manager role and my intention might be to do more of the talking.

Intention Tool: The "Tweet This" Approach

Less is more. You have 140 characters available on Twitter to communicate. Use a similar approach to get to the core of your intention. (That was 135 characters!)

Secondary Intentions (SI)

Your Laser-Focused Intention (LFI) should be your primary intention. However, you can also have multiple intentions for a communication.

I break it down as follows:

1. Your Primary Intention (PI) usually is more about the task, outcome, or result you're trying to accomplish by having this communication.

2. Your Secondary Intention (SI) is usually more about the person or relationship and the areas you need to focus on with the person to achieve the PI.

For example, imagine that as a manager, you are having a meeting with a new employee to give him or her some feedback on his or her performance. He or she is doing a good job and you have a few learning opportunities you want to discuss. Your PI is to give them feedback. Since he or she is new, you also want to make sure you have a few other intentions for the conversation. Therefore, you will also have some SI's for this conversation. Your SI's might be: 1. Educate, 2. Encourage, or 3. Build and maintain the relationship.

I believe every communication should have a SI of building and maintaining relationships. In order to have a true and meaningful impact on others, you must first establish a strong relationship.

The following tool will help you better understand and explore this concept.

Intention Tool: PI and SI

Think of a recent conversation you had with someone. Did you have a PI?

What were your SI's? Write an example of a Primary Intention (PI) and some Secondary Intentions (SI).

PI = _____

SI1 = _____

SI2 = _____

INTENTION

MESSAGE

PERSON

ACTIVATE

CLARIFY

TRANSFORM

Align Your Communication to Your Mission

Your company's mission statement is its PI. This is the intention your company has set for itself.

As an employee, it is important to keep this intention in mind as you perform your job. Therefore, whenever planning a communication, think about your company's mission statement and ask yourself, "Could this be one of my secondary intentions for my communication?" This will also help you stay congruent with your company's Primary Intention.

However, what I have found is that many employees are not familiar enough with their organization's mission statement even to consider using it as a secondary intention when planning their communication.

Recently, in one of my workshops, I asked the audience, "How many of your organizations have a mission statement?" I would say almost every hand in the room went up.

I followed up with another question, "How many of you could recite it to me right now?" Less than ten percent of the audience members raised their hands.

If your company wants to achieve their mission, then their employees should be familiar with their mission statement. The intention of your company should be an integral part of your everyday communication externally and internally. This could be your vision statement, mission, goals, and values – decide on whatever term you like, and then describe and disseminate that intention to all of the members of your organization.

Whenever possible, consider accomplishing your organization's mission statement as one of your Secondary Intentions (SI).

SUMMARY - Intention

This first principle, Intention, is a simple yet powerful key to communicating with IMPACT. It is the foundation for your communication and it only takes 30 seconds to craft, yet many people never take the time to do it.

If you have a Problem-Focused Intention, it could drive your communication down a negative path. So craft your Laser-Focused Intention (LFI) to make sure you are headed in the right direction.

Your intention is like your own internal GPS. It helps you stay focused on the outcome or destination of your communication.

You can have more than one intention for a communication. Your primary intention focuses on the task or result and your secondary intentions focus on the person you are communicating with to accomplish the outcome.

So the next time you find yourself in a conversation that is heading in the wrong direction or a communication that is taking you longer than you like, stop and take 30 seconds to check your Intention.

In the next section, Message, we will discuss how to make your Intention a reality.

> *"Communication starts with intention—as your intentions will be felt long before your message is heard."*
>
> *— Doug Firebaugh*

At the end of each chapter, I will give you a few tools to help you better understand the principle and apply it:

- "Impact Insights" you can ponder and share.
- "Coaching Reflection Questions" you can use to help you reflect and prepare to apply the principle.
- "Application" list of areas where you will apply this principle in the coming week.

Impact Insight (Intention)

Here are a few insights from this chapter. Which ones do you want to focus on this week?

Every time you communicate, there is an Intention behind it... whether or not you plan it.

Laser-Focused Intention: I am going to communicate with (Person) about (Message) so that they will (Intention/Result/Action) by (Transform).

The clearer your Intention is, the clearer your message will be.

Your Intention drives your conversation and your conversation drives the results you achieve.

If you start with a planned outcome, you increase your chance of achieving your Intention.

You can have more than one Intention for a communication. Your Primary Intention (PI) focuses on the task or result and your Secondary Intentions (SI) focus on the person you are communicating with to accomplish the outcome.

INTENTION

MESSAGE

PERSON

ACTIVATE

CLARIFY

TRANSFORM

Impact Reflection (Intention)

Ask these questions to help you better understand how to craft your Intention and your communication:

"If I only had 30 seconds, what would I want them to know, think, feel, or do?"

"What is my Intention for this communication?"

"What is the issue or challenge?" (and focus on results, not activities).

"Why am I having this communication with this person?"

"What is my strategic Intention?"

"As a result of the communication, what do I want the other person to think, do, or feel?"

"What is my purpose for communicating?"

"What roles do I play? Do I have a clear idea of my Intention for the roles? How does my role Intention affect my communication while playing that role?"

"What am I trying to achieve/accomplish through this communication?"

"What are my desired outcomes?"

"Where do I want to go with this conversation?"

Impact Application (Intention)

Below are lists of various situations where you may want to apply the Intention principle in your daily routine. Pick one or two that are applicable to you and your team. Then list a person, situation, and time wherein you want to apply this principle.

Presentation (examples: Staff meeting, committee update, board report, training seminar, speech, etc.)

Person: _____

Situation: _____

Date to Apply Principle: _____

Interpersonal Communication (examples: Conversation, phone call, luncheon, etc.)

Person: _____

Situation: _____

Date to Apply Principle: _____

Marketing/Sales Communication (examples: Sales call, luncheon, presentation, etc.)

Person: _____

Situation: _____

Date to Apply Principle: _____

Public Communication (examples: social media, radio/television interviews, video conferences, etc.)

Person: _____

Situation: _____

Date to Apply Principle: _____

INTENTION

MESSAGE

PERSON

ACTIVATE

CLARIFY

TRANSFORM

Message (mes'ij) – noun

a communication passed or sent by speech, in writing, by signals, etc.

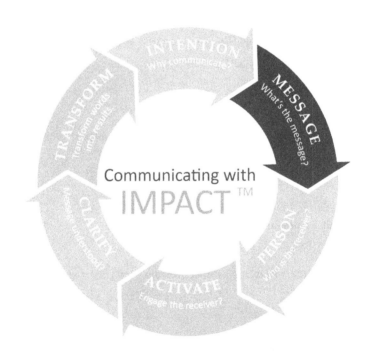

Principle 2

MESSAGE

- Interpersonal Communication Components
- First Impressions Open The Relationship Door
- It's Not Just What You Say
- The 7/38/55 Mehrabian Rule
- The 33/33/33/Donadio Rule
- Theory of Communication Preference
- Planning What to Say
- Five Tools to Craft Your Message
    1. Tool #1: Getting to Know You
    2. Tool #2: Mind Map – Non-Linear Approach
    3. Tool #3: Organize Your Message
    4. Tool #4: Designing Your Message
    5. Tool #5: Delivering the Message
- IMPACT Insight
- IMPACT Reflection
- IMPACT Application

INTENTION
MESSAGE
PERSON
ACTIVATE
CLARIFY
TRANSFORM

Principle 2

MESSAGE

*"Remember it is not just what you say,
it's also how you say it."*

M is for Message

What is the message? The message is what we say, write, or otherwise communicate both verbally and non-verbally. This message helps us to achieve our intention.

Now that you have your Laser-Focused Intention, it is time to craft the Message for your communication in a way to achieve the desired intention.

You cannot not communicate! We are always communicating whether you intend to or not. We should carefully craft our message and choose the appropriate method of delivery so that we communicate the message to the Receiver to achieve your intention and create the desired impact.

Did you know that even before you open your mouth you are sending a message to the receiver?

On a hot July day in 1990, I found myself on the way to prison. It was there that I experienced firsthand the power of the unspoken word.

I didn't know what to expect. I had never been to prison before and many thoughts were swirling in my head.

How safe is this place? How will they treat me? Will they like me?

I had never volunteered with youth before, let alone those who were incarcerated. The real reason I volunteered to join our church group was that a few of my friends who were going invited me. Now I was having second thoughts.

That is where I met Toby, a 14-year-old who was recently sent to juvenile detention. He would teach me an important lesson about the power of the unspoken word.

I had just finished playing cards with a small group of boys and I got up to meet some of the others when I spotted Toby. He was a reserved young man now sitting all by himself, hunched over and not making eye contact with anyone.

So I walked over and sat next to Toby. He sat there motionless. "Hi, my name is Pat. What's yours?"

"Toby," he whispered. I had to lean in to hear what he was saying.

"Did you have fun playing cards?" I asked.

"I guess so," he answered as he stared at the floor.

"This is my first time here. How long have you been here?" I asked in hopes to get him talking.

"Just about a week," he replied. He seemed even more nervous, but I kept going.

"So how are things?" I asked.

"Okay," he muttered.

I just paused, took a bite of my cookie, and waited. It seemed like forever, but in a few moments he started talking.

"I really miss my grandma," he said with a hint of sadness in his voice. "I live with her now."

"You do?" I asked, hoping to keep him talking.

"Yes. You see, when I was ten, my father abused me, and so they sent me to a boys' home to get away from my drug-addict dad and my alcoholic mom. Then my grandma took me in and I have been with her ever since."

"I am very sorry to hear that," I said. His next response startled me.

"Don't pity me!" he shouted with a tone of anger and fear.

I was caught off guard by his outburst. Here I thought I was being empathetic, but evidently he had not perceived my communication the same way.

I quickly changed the subject and a few minutes later, Toby started to tell me about "blanket parties."

"What are blanket parties?" I asked.

"Well, they usually happen at night, and that is when they throw a blanket over you and beat you up." Wow, I thought. This must be terrifying for him.

Toby was not the smallest kid in his group, but he sure looked like a victim; always looking down, not making eye contact, and walking slumped over.

"So how often do the blanket parties happen?" I asked, with genuine concern in my voice.

"Almost every night," he replied.

"Why do you think they pick on you?" I asked.

"I don't know. Why do you think they pick on me?" he mumbled.

Now I was in a quandary. Did he really want to know my thoughts, or was he being sarcastic? I decided to take a risk and tell him what I thought, "Well, to me you look like a victim."

I waited for his response, worried that I might have upset him.

"What do you mean?" he asked.

I explained, "Look at your body posture; you are slouched over, you don't make much eye contact, and you talk in a low tone. You give the impression that you are an easy target."

He looked at himself as if he was trying to see what I was talking about. In the meantime, I was thinking I had a few suggestions, but wasn't sure if I should share them.

Since the group leader told us our intention for being here was to minister to these fellow youths, I decided to share my suggestions. "Toby, I have a few suggestions for you. Would you like to hear them?" He looked up as I said this and nodded.

I continued, "Why don't you stop looking like a victim? Stand tall, look people in the eyes, and speak louder. Try not to look so victim-like. In fact, just try acting more confident."

He looked at me and said nothing. I thought, Now I did it. I really offended him. Then before either of us could say anything, our group leader gathered us all together to join in our closing prayer.

After the closing prayer, we started to pack up. Many of the boys were talking to the volunteers, thanking them and even giving them hugs. I saw Toby coming towards me as well. What is he going to do now? I thought to myself, apprehensively.

He came over to me, and in his quiet voice, said, "Thank you for coming tonight."

I said, "You are welcome," and I reached out my hand to shake his.

He took my hand and then pulled me in for a big bear hug. I was shocked.

"Thanks again," he said.

Well, the next month I saw Toby again. As he walked over to me, I noticed he looked different. He was making more eye contact, standing straight, and even his voice sounded more confident.

"Listen, I wanted to thank you for your advice last month," he blurted out.

"What was that?" I said.

"You know, your advice about looking like a victim," he said with a slight smile. "I started changing my body posture, eye contact, and attitude. Once I did this, I noticed the guys started to treat me differently." He continued, "And about a week after your last visit, the blanket parties stopped."

"Wow, that is good news!" I replied. Then we both went over to the snack table to get some cookies and orange soda.

As I left that night, I was amazed at what I learned. By changing his non-verbal communication, Toby was able to communicate a different message to the other boys and that resulted in a change in their behavior toward him.

Let's take a closer look at what really makes up your message.

M is for Message

Once you are clear about the intention for your communication, then you have to craft and communicate your message in a way to achieve the intention. You can do this through of variety of methods: the spoken word, the written word, pictures, videos, and so on.

Every time you interpersonally communicate (face-to-face) with people, you share a message and it has three components:

1. Your words

2. Your voice

3. Your non-verbal communication

Ideally, all three of these will come together into one message to help you

achieve your intention.

In the following box, take a minute and estimate what percentage of your interpersonal message comes from words, what percentage comes from voice, and what percentage comes from non-verbal elements? Again, think in general terms regarding face-to-face conversations.

Interpersonal Communication Components

When you communicate face-to-face, there are three parts to your message. They add up to 100%. Take a moment and fill in your guess at the breakdown:

_____ % comes from your Words

_____ % comes from your Voice

_____ % comes from your Non-verbals

100%

Later in this chapter, look to see how your estimates compare with the outcome of a UCLA study.

Interpersonal Communication — First Impressions Open the Relationship Door

When you meet someone, they form an impression of you—literally in seconds.

In fact, some studies say that it takes only about seven seconds for someone to form an impression of you.

In Toby's case, the other boys saw his non-verbal demeanor and formed the impression that he was an easy target. This impression led to how they treated him.

What about you? Are you conscious that people are forming an impression of you in seconds? Many times this initial impression has more to do with how you look: your clothes, body posture, grooming, eye contact, and so on, rather than what you say.

For example, you walk into an interview, you meet someone for lunch, you get up to present to the board, you have a one-on-one meeting with your boss...in every one of these situations, your first impression is going to influence the communication and how you interact will affect your message.

"A first impression is your strongest impression."

— Danielle Turcola, Image Consultant/Speaker

We should all strive to make a positive first impression because this starts the relationship off on the right foot. If you are unprepared for a conversation with a new person, and you happen to come off as unorganized or not confident, it might take many positive, confident encounters before that person ever sees you as a true professional, if ever.

The Great Communicator

If you look at recent presidents of the United States, they all have speech-writers to help them craft their message. However, what made them great were not just the words they used, but also how they delivered them.

President Ronald Reagan had the uncanny ability to connect with the American people. Because of his oratory skills, he was dubbed the Great Communicator. After his eight years as president, Ronald Reagan addressed the nation from the Oval Office on January 11, 1989. In his farewell address, President Reagan talked about this nickname: "I won a nick-name, the Great Communicator. But I never thought it was my style or the words I used that made a difference. It was the content."

Well, I hate to disagree with the late president, but it was also his style. I believe it is a combination of content and delivery. I have coached quite a few leaders, from CEOs to executive directors to college presidents, and the one common denominator that I have seen in all these various leaders was their need to improve delivery. Yes, content is important, but so is delivery.

It's not just what you say

I always look forward to watching the national presidential conventions and listening to all the speeches. Over the past few decades, two speakers really stood out for me. One was Mario Cuomo when he gave the keynote speech at the 1984 Democratic National Convention in San Francisco. The other was Barack Obama in 2004.

Mario Cuomo's delivery of that 1984 speech was inspiring. The way he used his voice to bring energy to his stories and examples, his pace and timing to bring emotion into his speech, the emphasis on key words to drive home his theme of the tale of two cities and family, and his overall delivery inspired me. In fact, it not only inspired me, it inspired many others and catapulted Cuomo into the national spotlight.

Fast-forward the clock twenty years. Another convention speaker caught my attention.

When I first saw then Illinois-State-Senator Obama give his speech at the 2004 Democratic National Convention in Boston, I thought to myself, this man has incredible passion and energy. You could see how he ignited and inspired the audience in front of him. I was impressed with his delivery. Little did I know that just four short years later he would be president of the United States.

Both speakers had put together a well-crafted speech, but it wasn't just what they said that inspired the audience; it was also how they said it.

Actions Speak Louder than Words

Early in my Communicating with IMPACT workshop, I ask people to estimate the percentage of their communication that comes from the words they say, their voice, and their non-verbal communication.

Before I give the audience the results of the study, I engage them in a simple exercise to model what I am about to tell them. I ask them all to stand up and play a quick game of "Follow the Leader." Through a series of commands, I have them repeat what I do. On the final command, I give them a conflicting message between what I tell them to do, my words, and what I do physically. Of course, a vast majority of the attendees follow my non-verbal behavior and not the words I used to describe the behavior.

They all chuckle. Once they experienced that it is not always the words that communicate the message. By making the audience experience this concept first, I have made them more open to the results of the study.

The 7/38/55 Mehrabian Rule

Professor Albert Mehrabian and his colleagues at UCLA conducted two studies in 1967 on communication patterns and published their results. Their study has drawn much controversy over the last half century since its publication due to its simple premise: when people communicate face-to-face, there are three parts to their message: words, voice, and non-verbal elements.

When we communicate feelings and attitudes, only 7% of our message comes from the words we use, according to Mehrabian.

38% of the message comes from your voice. Your tone, inflection, and pace, as well as countless other factors related to your enunciation of the message are just over 1/3 of the meaning.

Moreover, if the UCLA study is correct, a whopping 55% of your message comes from non-verbal elements, such as hand gestures, posture, facial expressions, and so forth.

The validity and importance of the Mehrabian 7/38/55 Rule has been taken out of context by speakers, consultants, and communication coaches over the years. They have applied it to all types of communication where it was not intended. In a 1994 article in Anchor Point, Mehrabian stated that he had never intended his results to be applied to normal conversations. He had only wanted to help his readers resolve incongruent messages regarding liking and disliking.

The Donadio Rule of Thirds

Based on my years of experience, I believe Mehrabian's research does have useful applications when taken with a grain of salt. I continue to use the three elements of the study in my speaking and training. These three components of interpersonal communication: word, voice, and non-verbal are present in our every day conversations. They might not exactly break down to 7/38/55 in terms of relative importance. However, given experience, I know that they exist in some mix.

For the sake of simplicity, let's just say all three are at least of equal importance – The Donadio Rule of Thirds:

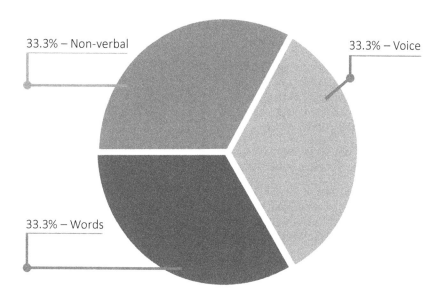

33.3% – Non-verbal

33.3% – Voice

33.3% – Words

I know they are not all equal but if they were, you can see that the voice and non-verbal components would account for 2/3 of the message. That leaves only 1/3 of the message coming from the words.

Yes, words are an important part of your face-to-face message. However, in some cases, words may be less important than we think. So remember to focus on the other two areas as well, your voice and your non-verbal behavior.

It is not just what you say; it's also how you say it!

Non-Verbal Communication - I am not old enough to drink coffee!

Growing up in an Italian family, we had plenty of non-verbal communication, especially with my immigrant grandparents. Since my grandparents lived close by (my mom's parents lived next door), I saw them often and I learned to communicate with them through non-verbal communication.

Both my grandmothers spoke the least English of the four grandparents. Since my grandfathers worked in the steel mills, they learned the language, but my grandmothers socialized mostly with family and other Italian immigrants. Although I understood some words in Italian, I was by no means fluent in the language. Many times I had to rely less on my limited understanding of the language (words) and focus on the tone and non-verbal part of the message.

For example, my grandmother (we called her Nana) might say, "Pat, vuoi un biscotto?" As she was asking me this in Italian, she would also make a hand gesture as if she was eating something. Of course, I knew what biscotti meant, and with the hand gestures, I realized she was asking if I was hungry and wanted a cookie.

One Sunday we were all sitting around the dinner table at Nana's house. Nana was serving coffee and her homemade pizzelles. I was the only kid at the table. She began by putting out the coffee cups to get ready to serve the coffee and placed one in front of me. When she did, I thought to myself, I am not old enough to drink coffee.

Well, she did not serve me coffee, but I will never forget what she did do. She served me milk in a coffee cup!

I really was not sure how to hold the cup because I had never drunk from a coffee cup before. However, when I looked around and saw my aunts and uncles drinking coffee out of the same cups, I realized that I felt included. It was special to be drinking out of the same china as the grown ups.

Why did Nana serve me milk in a coffee cup? She could have easily given me a glass. This was her way of making me feel part of the group. Not a word was spoken, yet the message was loud and clear.

Theory of Communication Preference

My grandparents preferred face-to-face communication. Since they could not speak English well, or read or write well, they preferred talking with you so they could use hand gestures and see your facial expressions to communicate.

My experience at Nana's house and communicating with my grandparents made me aware that certain people responded well to one mode of communication versus another.

As I moved into the working world, I also began to pay more attention to which mode of communication people responded to best.

Certain people would respond very quickly to an email or a text message but would take forever to respond to my voicemail message, while others would not respond well to email, but respond quickly to a phone call. Even others would not respond well to a phone call or an email, but would respond faster to a text message.

In 1992, the first text message was sent. Today, the number of texts sent each year exceeds the world's population.

What is Your Communication Preference?

Assign each of the preferences on the next page a percentage of your total communication. Then look on the page after that for results by generation in a similar 2010 survey.

IMPACT Insight: Communication Preference

Message	Rank Preference
Interpersonal (face-to-face)	%
Presentation (to group)	%
Telephone call (landline or VOIP)	%
Cell phone call (mobile)	%
Video conferencing	%
Text message	%
Paper letter	%
Handwritten note	%
Fax	%
Email	%
Tweet	%
Facebook	%
LinkedIn	%
Blogging	%
Other (explain)	%
TOTAL	100 %

What is Your Co-worker's/Prospect's/Client's Communication Preference?

You can also use the grid to rank others' preferences.

Today we have more ways to communicate than ever before. However, we are not changing the message; we are simply changing the medium.

Start paying attention to the people with whom you communicate and begin to see if you can tell which communication preferences they have.

Also, just because they have a certain preference does not mean that should be your final and only mode of communication with them, but it would be a great place to start.

If you are lucky, you'll come across people who will tell you their communication preference. Instead of waiting, simply ask people for their preference.

Communication by Generation

Based on BIGresearch® Simultaneous Media Survey (SIMM17)

Message	Gen Y	Gen X	Boomer	All
Face-to-Face	62.9%	69.5%	68.0%	65.7%
Email	44.6%	54.1%	54.8%	52.4%
Cell phone	54.5%	42.0%	31.4%	36.8%
Telephone (landline)	21.9%	27.5%	37.1%	32.2%
Text Messaging	44.0%	31.7%	15.4%	24.3%
Instant Messaging	37.7%	19.2%	8.4%	16.8%
Social Media	38.1%	24.7%	11.2%	19.6%
Blogging	15.5%	7.4%	2.3%	6.3%
Other	0.9%	1.2%	2.3%	2.2%

Dec. 2010

IMPACT Tip: Reader/Writer Leader

If a Receiver is a reader, you should write to them.

If a Receiver is a listener, then you should tell them.

Lead with their preference! Then follow up using the other medium.

Planning What to Say

Whether you are meeting with a co-worker, having a phone call with an important customer, sending an e-mail proposal, making a sales presentation, or even delivering a video conference, the key to making an impact with your communication is to spend some time planning what you want to say.

Planning and structuring your message will not only help you, it also helps the receiver understand your message better.

I happened to be on the radio just before Thanksgiving, talking about the importance of being an effective communicator and promoting my audiocassette program called "Communicating with IMPACT" (yes, I said audiocassette, it was the early 1990s). When the host asked me about tips for planning and organizing your ideas, I answered, "In the spirit of Thanksgiving, let me share a formula that I use to organize my ideas." Then, I quipped: "Know your stuff, know who you are stuffing, and stuff them!"

As a member of Toastmasters International, an organization committed to helping people improve their communication and leadership skills, I learned the phrase, "Tell them what you are going to tell them, tell them, and then tell them what you told them."

No matter how you look at it, when crafting your message, keep in mind that every communication has the three main components:

1. Opening

2. Body

3. Closing

Five Tools to Craft Your Message

Planning is an important part of the Communicating with IMPACT process. Sometimes the planning is formal and other times it is informal.

These tools here work for all the types of communication we discussed. Since I specialize in interpersonal communication, I will use these areas as examples.

Here are five tools to help you plan your message:

Tool #1: Getting to Know You – HW5

In journalism class at Ohio University, the professor taught us the HW5 method. These are the key questions you want to ask when developing a news story or preparing to interview a guest on your show. This method works for crafting any type of message. The six questions are: How, Who, What, When, Where, and Why.

Here are some examples of the HW5 method in action:

• How will you know if this is successful?

• Who is the receiver? (age, gender, education....)

• What is the receiver's background? (training, experience, knowledge level, etc.)

• When will they expect the conversation to be done?

- Where is the organization headed in the next 12 months?

- Why are they attending this meeting?

All this information is crucial to help you craft the message and deliver the message to the receiver.

The Sixth "W"

There is also a sixth "W" that I did not learn in my journalism classes. The all-important sixth W is: Who cares?

The message is more about the receiver and less about you. We may think we are important, but what really matters is the receiver. As you are crafting the message, ask yourself, "Who cares?"

As you prepare your message, keep in mind the sixth "W" question: Who cares? Many times we think that an idea, example, or story is important to include in the message. By asking, "Who cares?" we are reminded to consider if this will be important for the overall message and the Receiver. If not, even if we think it will add to the message, it may be better to leave it out.

In order to be able to answer this question, you have to do your homework. Find out as much as possible to better help you craft the message.

Do Your Homework

Gather and learn far more than you will ever use. Your preparation could include: research, reading (newspapers, magazines, journals, websites, and so on), interviewing people, reflecting on your own experience, and knowing your Receiver!

In terms of doing your Receiver analysis, I think about analyzing the Receiver the moment someone asks me about an issue, gives me a task, or invites me to make a presentation. This is your first level of research.

For example, when someone invites you to speak or present, this is the perfect opportunity to start your research. The first person who invites you is the initial "meeting planner."

When the "meeting planner" says, "I would like for you to come and present at our meeting on Monday," you reply, "I am happy to, but may I ask you a few questions?" Look at the HW5 method discussed previously and begin to ask some questions to identify every reason or "intention" for having you present.

INTENTION
MESSAGE
PERSON
ACTIVATE
CLARIFY
TRANSFORM

Here are a few other questions you can ask:

- What are the top three challenges this group is facing?

- What is your goal or intention for this event?

- If you are going to make this presentation, will you tell them?

- What do you want them to think, do, or feel at the end of my presentation?

- Whom else do you recommend I talk with to learn more about this group?

If you are doing a presentation where you do not know in advance who will be in the audience, I suggest you try a more informal, just-in time approach. Get to the event early to mingle with the crowd before you present. I find that I can learn quite a lot about the group by just walking around, meeting people, and asking them questions.

The more you sweat in advance,
the less you will sweat on stage!

Mind Map Template

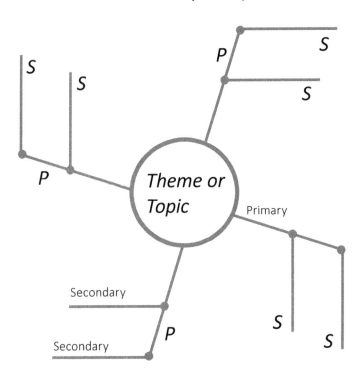

To download more IMPACT resources, go to http://www.Patrick Donadio.com

Tool #2: Mind Map – Non-Linear Approach

When most people start to think about crafting or outlining a message, they take out a piece of paper or start typing their ideas out in a linear fashion: What do I say first? Second? Third? How should I close?

This linear approach can stifle your creativity and even cause you to get stuck. I suggest that you try using a non-linear approach. One way to create your message is to use a tool like the mind map. The goal here is just to get all your ideas out on paper without judging them.

So if you are stuck, draw a diagram like the one on the previous page to map your ideas.

Mind Map Directions

1. In the center circle, write down your theme or Laser-Focused Intention (LFI). Again, you can use the LFI structure: "I am going to talk to _____ (Receiver) about _____ (Topic) so they will _____ (Action)."

2. Then on the Primary spokes (the long lines coming off the main circle), write down whatever comes to mind about this topic.

Do not worry about the order or even if you will use the ideas. You want to get all your ideas out on paper first and then you can look at structure, order, and whether or not you will use the ideas.

3. Once you have filled the Primary spokes, you now want to go back and look at each Primary line and start expanding that line into various components (Secondary points) or issues you would like to cover for each Primary point by filling in the secondary, smaller perpendicular lines. Again, do not worry about order or relevance. The goal is to creatively come up with ideas. Later you will process the ideas and decide what to keep or use.

4. Now that you have completed the map, the final phase is to start looking at lines and begin to think linearly. Rank your points in the order you want to present them:

    1. Place numbers (1, 2, 3, 4...) by the Primary spoke to indicate what order you want to present these points.

    2. Next, look at the Secondary spokes, sub-lines, and delete or move these around to main lines until you feel they make sense to you and your receiver. You can also place numbers here to begin thinking about the order.

    3. Now take out a clean piece of lined paper and write out your outline in standard outline form. For example:

1. Primary – Developing Confidence
2. Secondary
    1. Some Fear is Useful
    2. Mental Preparation
    3. Monitor Self Talk
    4. Rehearse and Practice
    5. _____?

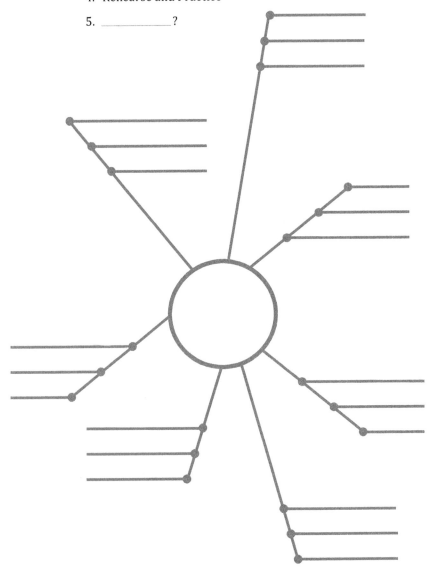

Tool #3: Organize Your Message - Linear Approach

Why Have Structure?

Structure is important for you as the creator of the message and for the Receiver(s) of your message.

Have you ever listened to someone share a concept and had no clue what he or she was trying to convey? There is a good chance they lacked structure to their communication.

Structure helps you organize the information so it leads to the achievement of your intention.

Structure captures the receiver's attention, keeps them engaged, and makes it easier for them to listen to and understand your message.

Finally, the message structure will help you organize the information in a way the makes it quicker and easier to deliver.

> *"In making a speech, one must study three points: first, the means of producing persuasion; second, the language; third, the proper arrangement of the various parts of the speech."*
>
> — *Aristotle*

Various Ways to Structure the Message

Every message has three main sections:

1. Opening

2. Body

3. Closing

Given this foundation, there are then various ways you can structure your presentation. Most of the structuring comes in the body of the message. Let's look at these three main areas.

Message - Opening

Whether you are writing an email, leaving a voicemail, or making a presentation, what you say or write in the first few moments sets the tone for the entire message.

Your opening has three important purposes:

1. To capture the Receiver's attention.

2. To establish rapport with the Receiver.

3. To introduce the content of the message.

To develop your opening, think about the Intention of your message. Use my Laser-Focused Intention (LFI) model from Chapter One. Now based on the LFI, what is the best way to introduce the message?

For example, if your LFI is to teach senior leaders about presentation skills so they can better deliver inspiring messages, then you might want to open with a story or question to get people thinking.

Opening Mistakes

There are varieties of ways to open your communication. Some people think that saying "Good Morning" is considered an opening. Others think that they should open with "Thank You."

We have all read e-mails or have been to presentations where someone started this way.

From my years of working with organizations and their people, one of the most common mistakes communicators make is not having a powerful opening.

Every day I read, see, or hear people using ineffective openings. Here are a few ways not to open.

- **No Trite Comments**

Imagine starting your communication with something as boring as:

"As requested, I am writing to you to discuss...."

"Good morning, ladies and gentleman, thank you for inviting me to speak with you today...."

Open with something different, unique, and attention getting! If you want to thank them, you can, just do it after your powerful opening.

- **A Slow Start**

Read the following text aloud, slowly, and in a monotone voice:

"Good afternoon, I am so excited to be here today. For the next two hours I will be showing you how to...."

By this point, most of the audience is already nodding off!

Open your presentation instead with enthusiasm and energy! (However, not too much – this can also be a bad thing.)

Very early in my speaking career I was invited to speak in Cincinnati, Ohio to a group of 400 older adults.

It was 7:30 in the morning and as the host was introducing me, I was backstage waiting with excitement to kick off this event.

As soon as the host mentioned my name, I briskly ran out in front of the audience and shouted very loudly with enthusiasm: "Good morning!"

Then suddenly, I heard a scream and a thump. There right in from of me, sitting on the floor in the front row was an older woman with her legs crossed and arms folded. Evidently, I scared her with my enthusiasm.

Now that was a poor opening. Always consider the balance and find the happy medium between overenthusiastic and boring.

- **An Apology**

Avoid starting with "I am sorry," especially when making a presentation.

"I am sorry the original speaker is ill and I was asked last night to present in her place...."

Avoid opening with an apology. If you need to apologize, do so later. Why bring attention to the issue, especially in the first few sentences or few minutes?

- **Clichés and Jokes**

An accountant steps on stage and says, "Ben Franklin said, 'A penny saved is a penny earned.'" Yawn! I am sure this accountant could have found a more creative quote to open his or her presentation on tax deductions.

If you are going to use quotes, try to find some that are unique and that others may not have heard before. In addition, be careful of only quoting dead white men like Ben Franklin! Have some variety in the quotes you use.

The problem with opening with a joke is you never know how many people have heard it before. "A guy walks into a bar and sees a talking frog...." This may be a fine joke, but it has nothing to do with the topic. Therefore, it is not a good opening.

A quote or joke can be used as a powerful opening as long as it does three things: captures the receiver's attention, introduces the content, and builds rapport with the receiver.

IMPACT Insight: Openings

Start watching how people Open their communication. Pay attention to the following points.

- How did the communicator open? Did he/she have a prepared opening?
- Does their opening meet my three criteria for a powerful opening:
  1. Does it capture your attention?
  2. Does it build rapport with you?
  3. Does it introduce the content?

Powerful Openings - What You Can Do

There are many ways to open that will capture the reader/audience's attention, build rapport, and introduce the content. In my workshop, I spend over an hour just talking about openings. Here are a few ways you can open:

- A story from your experience
- A startling statement
- An interesting statistic
- A question
- A quote
- Audience participation (involve them physically, mentally, and/or emotionally)
- A prop, photo, or visual

IMPACT Tip: Craft Your Opening Last

Finally, consider crafting your opening last. Your opening is supposed to introduce the message to the reader/listener. How can you introduce the message until you know what the message is going to be?

Once you know what you are going to say, then you can plan the best way to introduce the presentation. I find that this ensures that my opening meets one of my three criteria, "introduce the content."

2. Message Body

The body of your message is where you will use the components from your mind map and put them in an order to help you make your intention a reality. Again, keep the intention for this speech in the forefront of your mind as you craft the message.

A focused message is a powerful message. Condense all the information into one to five main points.

Here are a few ways you can structure these main components:

- From Past to Present to Future
- From Future to Present
- Question and Answer
- Chronological by Time
- From Least to Most Important
- From Most to Least Important
- From General to Specific
- Pros vs. Cons
- Cause and Effect
- Challenge and Solution
- Pain and Remedy

INTENTION

MESSAGE

PERSON

ACTIVATE

CLARIFY

TRANSFORM

What other ways can you think of to structure your presentation? Write a few possibilities in the spaces below.

_____

_____

_____

_____

Remember to have supporting information like examples, stories, statistics, quotes, and so forth, in addition to the facts for each main point. You will learn more about this when I discuss how to activate your message.

IMPACT Insight: Structure

Start watching how people Structure their communication. Pay attention to the following points.

- Did they have an opening?
- Could you identify the main point(s) of the communication?
- Did they structure the content?
- If so, what type of format did they use to structure the presentation?
- Did they have a closing?

3. Message Closing

The closing is an important part of the message. This is your last chance to make sure that the message you sent is the same message they received.

This is true in written as well as in spoken communication.

I have seen some poor presentations salvaged by a great close and some great presentations ruined by a poor close.

More often than not, I find that many people have either no closing or a poor closing. I was guilty of this early on in my career.

I remember my first paid speech; I was so nervous that when I was done speaking, I just stopped and stood there waiting for applause. I did not even say the proverbial thank you. Finally after about 15 seconds, which to me felt like an eternity, the introducer walked up and started the applause.

I learned a valuable lesson that day: wrap up your communication with a closing and, when speaking, preferably a closing that you prepare in advance.

The closing could include one or all of the following:

1. Review or summary.

2. Call to action.

3. Closing statement using the 30-Second Rule.

4. Review or Summary

A rule of thumb is: the longer the communication, the more important the summary.

Don't review all the main points; cover a few highlights that really capture the intent of the message and lead into your final closing that will help you make the intention of your message a reality.

5. Call to Action

The next possible part of your closing could be the call to action. Is your intent of the message to get the receiver to do something? Ask yourself this question to find out: "What do you want the receiver to do as a result of this message?" If you come up with an answer that says, you want the receiver to do, approve, accept, explore, analyze, and so on, in the closing you might want to ask the receiver to act.

Do not assume the receiver knows that they are supposed to do something. Ask or tell them to transform the intent into action. I will talk more about this in the Transform chapter.

6. Dynamic Closing Statement

The closing statement is a brief way to sum up your message, leave the receiver/audience with a clear understanding of your message, and, if appropriate, focus on what you want them to think, feel, or do as a result of listening to you.

You can actually close with some of the same techniques you used to open—for example, with a story from your experience, a startling statement or statistic, a prop, photo, or video, a quote, and so on.

When it comes to closing your communication, I recommend that you come prepared with a closing statement and rehearse it so you can deliver it without using any notes.

Most of the time I find the intent for the closing statement is to leave a positive impression. However, there are always exceptions. Research shows that we are motivated by two elements: pain or pleasure. We will take action when we experience either pain or pleasure. When the pain or pleasure is great enough, we will take action.

It goes back to the carrot and the stick example I learned in college. You can motivate the donkey by using the stick and hitting the animal and coercing it to move forward. Alternatively, you can motivate it by dangling a carrot on the stick in front of the donkey and luring it forward.

Use The 30 Second Rule to Craft Your Closing

In the Intention Chapter, we talked about the 30-Second Rule to help you uncover the intention for the message. You can use this same tool to help you craft your closing statement.

Ask yourself, "If I only had 30 seconds to communicate this message what would I tell them?"

Now take this core message and craft your closing. You can close with some of the same techniques you opened with: a story, a startling statement, a quote, a final thought, etc. The difference is that the closing's purpose is to leave them with a final message that sums up your intention for this communication.

I was coaching a high-level physician as he was preparing to speak on behalf of a healthcare consortium about the results of their recent combined efforts regarding improving patient safety. His original closing line was: "We are very grateful for the support of all these partners who recognize the importance of focusing on Every Patient, Every Day."

Yes, he had a closing. However, when I asked him if this closing achieved his intent for this brief presentation, he responded, "No, I think it is missing something."

So I then asked him the question, "If you only had 30 seconds to communicate this message, what would you want to say?"

He responded with, "Since 2005, we have been collaborating to improve quality and patient safety. Our efforts have translated into saving more lives and millions of dollars every year in our region."

Armed with this new information, we reworked his closing and here is what we came up with:

"We are very grateful for the support of all our partners. And with your continued efforts we will further reduce the costs of healthcare and save even more lives in our region by focusing on Every Patient, Every Day."

You can see the new closing left a clearer vision and a positive impression.

Final Closing Tip

Whenever possible, never close with a Question & Answer session. This puts the control of your final impression in the hands of the audience. If you are asked some negative questions, the mood of the audience may be tainted by this.

Come back after Q & A with a final closing that will leave them with the tone you intended, instead of the tone the audience may set.

IMPACT Insight: Closings

Start watching how people Close their communication. Pay attention to the following points.

- Did he/she have a prepared closing?
- Did the speaker close on Q&A?
- What was the overall impression you had when you left the presentation?
- Do you know what the speaker wants you to do? Think? Feel?

Tool #4: Designing Your Message

Now that you have done your research, fleshed out your ideas, and created a structure, it is time to design the message. I am not going to spend much time on message writing, but I do want to talk about how to design your message to inspire action and to transform these actions into the achievement of your original intention.

TIP 1 - Use Benefit Language

In my early days of speaking, I learned something important called "features versus benefits" language. For example, if you are going to buy a new car and the salesperson informs you that the car you are looking at has the cruise control as one of its features, you probably say (or at least think) something like, "Why do I need cruise control? Who cares?"

The salesperson at that point proceeds to pitch you the benefits of cruise control.

"With cruise control you can set the speed at 65 mph and you can avoid the chance of getting a speeding ticket. If you set the cruise control at 65 mph, a consistent speed will give you better gas mileage. By using cruise control on a long trip, you can eliminate the need to constantly hold down the accelerator and reduce your chance of getting a leg cramp."

The term "cruise control" does not adequately explain why I would need or want this item. The benefits are what truly convince me to purchase the car with this feature. The same is true when you are crafting your message. When appropriate, explain to the receiver what's in it for them.

Explain to the receiver how you can help them do the following: save time, save money, increase income, decrease expenses, reduce stress, reduce risk, improve efficiency, feel better, work faster, look better, be safer, save lives…. What others can you think of?

TIP 2 - Communicate the Benefits

As you design your message, always remember to explain the benefits to the receiver.

Going back to the example I gave of the high-level physician who was preparing to speak on behalf of a healthcare consortium, remember how we reshaped his closing to emphasize the benefits? He originally closed his presentation by saying, "Recognize the importance of focusing on Every Patient, Every Day."

We reworked his closing to add the following statement that emphasized the benefits of what he was pitching: "We are very grateful for the support of all our partners. And with your continued efforts we will further reduce the costs of healthcare and save even more lives in our region by focusing on Every Patient, Every Day."

Features	Benefits
Cruise Control	Saves gas mileage
Focus on the patient	Reduce errors, save lives
_____	_____
_____	_____

Those few extra words detailing the benefits to the receiver (reduce costs and saving even more lives) made all the difference for him as he communicated with his audience.

Now think about a message that you are trying to convey and list some of the features. See if you can convert them into benefits.

TIP 3 - "You" vs. "I" Language

Design the message with the receiver in mind.

The more "I" words you have in the message, the more the message appears to be focused on the sender and less on the receiver. So pay attention to the balance of "You" and "I."

Pay attention to the "You" versus "I" ratio. You will want to use more "You" statements whenever possible.

However, when having a one-on-one conversation to address a stressful or controversial situation, keep in mind that "You" statements can make the other person feel defensive, judged, controlled, threatened, and criticized. "I" statements are generally more descriptive, encouraging, egalitarian, and problem-focused.

IMPACT Insight: "You" versus "I" Language

Pay greater attention to your use of "I" versus "You" language, especially in one-on-one communication. Which word do you use more often? "You" statements can sometimes make the other person feel judged or defensive.

Can you change the "You" statement into an "I" statement?

Avoid "You" Statements	Use "I" Statements
"You should...."	"I was expecting that...."
"You need to...."	"I encourage you to...."
"You have to...."	"I would like you to...."
"You are always...."	"When you...I feel...."
"You are wrong."	"I see there is a misunderstanding."
"You are confusing me."	"Maybe I misunderstood."
"You can't do that."	"I would like to help if I can."

INTENTION

MESSAGE

PERSON

ACTIVATE

CLARIFY

TRANSFORM

Use more "You" statements in presentations and more "I" statements in stressful or difficult conversations. Here are some examples:

In Stressful or Controversial Situations

Pay greater attention to your use of "I" versus "You" language. See which word you use more often, and how you can change the "You" statement into an "I" statement when giving feedback or dealing with a difficult situation.

TIP 4 – Avoid Speaking "Down"

When I have to travel, I like to reward myself with a special coffee. I usually order a decaf, triple medium, skinny, wet, cappuccino with legs. For those of you who do not frequent the specialty coffee chains that I do, my order is probably confusing. But the barista with whom I speak immediately understands from my lingo that I just ordered a decaf, medium with three shots of espresso (triple medium), with non-fat milk (skinny), and more milk than foam (wet), cappuccino, to go (with legs).

Many organizations have acronyms and internal jargon that can be confusing to an outsider. Be sure to avoid using the lingo with outsiders, or if you have to use it, be sure to explain each expression for those who may not be familiar with your internal cultural code.

TIP 5 – Explain the "Why" Behind the Message

People want to know the reasons behind what they are being asked to do. Not explaining the "why" often means employees won't be engaged with what you are saying. By taking the time to explain why something needs to be done, you create an atmosphere of understanding and engagement. The more engaged, the better result.

During these challenging and hectic times, after you communicate a decision, a new policy, or a change in existing procedures, take a few minutes and explain the "why" behind the decision.

Tool #5: Delivering the Message

While crafting your message, you still want to give some thought to the delivery.

To do this, ask yourself the following questions:

- "How will I bring this message to life?"
- "How will I keep the receiver engaged?"

- "How do I make sure the message I send is the same one they receive?"

- "How do I say this so it is pulling them into my conversation and not pushing them away?"

TIP 1 - Start Paying Attention to the Tone

Pay attention to the tone of your message. How are you coming across verbally and non-verbally? How do you want to come across?

Are you friendly or irritated, strong or weak, patient or frustrated, confident or helpless? Are you trusting or distrustful, excited or disappointed, hopeful or worried, comfortable or uncomfortable, interested or bored? Are you open or closed-minded, connected or aloof, grateful or guilty, superior or inferior, appreciative or ungrateful?

Before you communicate, spend some time in the planning stage to focus on how you will be congruent nonverbally. Go back, revisit your Laser-Focused Intention (LFI) for this communication, and ask yourself:

- "What tone should I use to best convey my message/intention (the words)?"

- "What body language should I use to best convey my message/intention (the words)?"

We can either push people toward something or pull them toward something. In my experience, both work. I am sure you have heard the example before about trying to push a rope versus pulling the rope. Both will work, but one takes more work (pushing), and because of the resistance, the other (pulling) is far more effective.

TIP 2 - Push vs. Pull Communication

Pushing is more direct.

When you are pushing, you feel like you have to make something happen. So you do more talking and convincing in order to push the person toward the message or outcome.

You might even find yourself using fear and coercion to communicate what you want.

Pulling is indirect.

When you are pulling, you feel like the other person can make it happen so you ask more questions and in turn attract the person toward the message or outcome.

When pulling people toward something, we tend to use more inquiry and engagement.

SUMMARY - Message

Crafting your message is the first principle to fulfilling your Intention. The second principle, Message, is where the real communication begins.

The message can be made up of both your words and your non-verbal communication. It all depends on the way you decide to craft and deliver your message.

Keep in mind that the receiver may have a preference as to how they want to receive your message. Choosing the appropriate delivery mechanism based on the content and the receiver will increase your chances of communicating with IMPACT.

When it comes to crafting your message, work smarter, not harder. The five tools in the section for crafting the message should help you create a more impactful message in less time.

In the next principle, Person, we will talk more about tailoring the message to the receiver.

IMPACT Insight (Message)

Here are a few insights from this chapter. Which ones do you want to focus on this week? Remember it is not just what you say, it is also how you say it.

Every time you interpersonally communicate (face-to-face), your message has three components: words, voice, and non-verbal communication.

When you meet someone, they form an impression of you—literally in seconds.

People have preferences for how they want you to communicate with them. Choose the best approach for each person. If they are a reader, write them, if they are a listener, tell them, and if they are visual, show them.

Know the Receiver. Use the HW5 method to learn more.

Use the Mind Map to craft an outline for your communication in less time.

Keep in mind that every communication has the three main components: an Opening, a Body, and a Closing.

Craft a powerful opening to capture the Receiver's attention, introduce the message, and build rapport.

As you design your message, always remember to explain the benefits to the receiver.

A focused message is a powerful message.

INTENTION

MESSAGE

PERSON

ACTIVATE

CLARIFY

TRANSFORM

IMPACT Reflection (Message)

Here are a few questions to help you better craft your Message and achieve the Intention you set for your communication:

"Am I conscious that people are forming an impression of me in seconds?"

"Do I match my behavior to my words?"

"Have I ever had someone treat me in a way that made me feel special? Included? Excluded? Confident? Inferior? What did he or she do?"

"Have I ever had a boss or co-worker walk by and give me a big smile? How did that make me feel?"

"What is my Co-worker's/Prospect's/Client's Communication Preference?"

"How will I adapt to their preference?"

When crafting a message for a presentation, ask yourself:

- What are the top three challenges the Receivers are facing?

- What is my goal or intention for this event?

- What do I want them to think, do, or feel at the end of my presentation?

"How did the communicator open? Did he/she have a prepared opening? Do I prepare my opening in advance?"

"What structure will I use to help the receiver stay engaged?"

"If I only had 30 seconds to communicate this message, what would I tell them?"

IMPACT Application (Message)

Below are lists of various situations where you may want to apply the Message principle in your daily routine. Pick one or two that are applicable to you and list a person, situation, and time when you want to apply this principle.

Presentation (examples: Staff meeting, committee update, board report, training seminar, speech, etc.)

Person: _____

Situation: _____

Date to Apply Principle: _____

Interpersonal Communication (examples: Conversation, phone call, luncheon, etc.)

Person: _____

Situation: _____

Date to Apply Principle: _____

Marketing/Sales Communication (examples: Sales call, luncheon, presentation, etc.)

Person: _____

Situation: _____

Date to Apply Principle: _____

Public Communication (examples: social media, radio/television interviews, video conferences, etc.)

Person: _____

Situation: _____

Date to Apply Principle: _____

INTENTION

MESSAGE

PERSON

ACTIVATE

CLARIFY

TRANSFORM

Person (pɥr'sən) – noun

a human being, esp. as distinguished from a thing or lower animal; individual man, woman, or child

personality; self; being

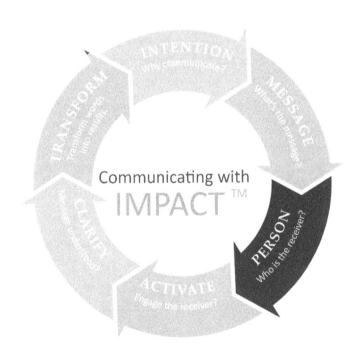

PRINCIPLE 3
Person

- The Golden Rule
- Alessandra's Platinum Rule®
- Identifying and Grouping Types of Human Behavior
- The DISC Model
- Four Behavioral Factors
- Introvert vs. Extrovert
- Task (Analytical) vs. Feeling (Relational)
- How You Can Improve Your DISC Style
- Personal Differences – What Gets in the Way?
- Individual vs. Group Differences
- Using the IMPACT Process
- IMPACT Insight
- IMPACT Reflection
- IMPACT Application

INTENTION

MESSAGE

PERSON

ACTIVATE

CLARIFY

TRANSFORM

PRINCIPLE 3
Person

"Be flexible. As a Sender, adapt and blend your communication style to the Receiver's style."

P is for Person

Who is the Receiver? Now that you have a clear Intention and have crafted a Message to achieve it, you should pay attention to the Person with whom you will be communicating, and how to personalize and tailor this message to the Receiver to get a better result.

This chapter explores the differences between you and the Receiver. The better we understand those differences and adjust, the more powerful the impact.

Have you every communicated with someone and felt that you were not connecting?

My client, John, is the CEO of a computer software company. In other words, he lives and operates in a world filled with numbers. When John and I first met, I sensed he was task-oriented, and he came across as very matter-of-fact. This was almost the exact opposite of my style—I am gregarious and talkative—so I had to adapt my outgoing, friendly, and verbose communication style to his more introverted, analytical, and matter-of-fact style.

In our first session, we got right to work. I asked John lots of questions to draw out information, help him analyze the problem at hand, and gain his trust. This worked well with John's straightforward, contemplative, and introverted style. John was aware of his need to polish his presentation skills, and that is why he asked me to help.

In our second session, I had John do a benchmark presentation and I video recorded it. As soon as John finished his presentation, and before we watched the video, I asked him a simple question to help him identify his perspective on the presentation, "John, how did you feel the presentation went?"

After I asked that question, I could sense that John was out of his element. He looked at me like a deer in the headlights. There was dead silence.

While waiting for John's response, I realized that I had asked John the wrong question. John is an analytical person and I had just asked him a "feeling" question, "How did you feel the presentation went?"

I projected onto John how I would like to be asked a question as an extroverted, feelings-oriented person. As an introverted, analytical person, John would naturally be drawn to a "thinking," not a "feeling" question.

As soon as I realized I had asked John the wrong question, I broke his silence with another, more personality-appropriate question, "John, let me ask that in a different way. How do you think the presentation went?"

Immediately, John perked up and began to describe to me, in detail, how he thought the presentation went.

By matching my Message to the style of the Receiver, I helped John bring his thoughts into focus.

The Golden Rule

We all know the Golden Rule, which is more or less worded as, "Do unto others as you would have them do unto you." The Golden Rule is a great rule to follow when talking about how to act and treat others. However, when it comes to communicating with others, the Golden Rule is not always the best rule.

Each of us is different and unique, and if we practice the Golden Rule in our communication, we follow the assumption that we are alike. Therefore, we treat people the way we want to be treated. If you have friends, have been in a relationship, are in a leadership position, or work on a team, it is clear that we are not all alike. That is why, when it comes to our communication, we should treat others as they want to be treated.

*"The most challenging part of building or being in a
relationship is coming to realize the other person is not you."*

— *Kevin Buck, CEO, Emergent Success*

Alessandra's Platinum Rule®

In his book, *The Platinum Rule*, Dr. Tony Allesandra lays out a different rule that takes into consideration the need to adapt our interactions and communication to the other person's preferences in order to build deeper relationships and more effectively communicate our message.

The Platinum Rule states: "Do unto others as they want done unto them."

Given *The Platinum Rule's* premise, let us explore different personalities and behaviors people possess from a variety of perspectives.

*"To effectively communicate, we must realize that we are
all different in the way we perceive the world and use this
understanding as a guide to our communication with others."*

— *Anthony Robbins*

Identifying and Grouping Types of Human Behavior

There are many ways to look at personality types and how people behave. Here are a few of the more common ones:

1. The Four Temperaments

From early history, we believed that people came from different personality types. In 400 B.C., the Greek philosopher Hippocrates came up with the theory that there were four temperaments based on the body fluids of black bile, yellow bile, blood, and phlegm. He called these four temperaments:

Melancholic (black bile)

Choleric (yellow bile)

Sanguine (blood)

Phlegmatic (phlegm)

Hippocrates believed these body fluids influenced personality. Each temperament had different characteristics.

2. The Four Mental Functions

In 1921, Swiss psychiatrist Carl Jung published his book *Psychological Types*. His work was based on the evidence of his years of working closely with hundreds of psychiatric patients. In his book, Jung proposed that people possess one of eight different psychological types, depending on four mental "functions": thinking, sensing, feeling, and intuition.

3. The Four Primary Emotions

In 1928, William Moulton Marston wrote *Emotions of Normal People*. In his book, he explored the behaviors of individuals in the environment. Marston wanted to study "normal" people as opposed to Jung's research based on the mentally ill. Marston studied the behaviors of individuals in their environment focused on the styles and preferences of their behaviors.

In his book, Marston identified four "primary emotions" and associated behavioral responses, which we know today as DISC.

DISC is an acronym for:

Dominance

Influence

Steadiness ("Submission" in Marston's original book)

Conscientiousness

I could go on and on with various other examples of personality types. From my perspective and experience, the DISC model (based on Marston's work) seems to be the quickest and easiest system to use.

I start every one of my one-on-one leadership communication coaching programs by doing a communication behavior profile (DISC) on the client to help me better understand them and thus better coach them. This jumpstarts our coaching relationship and reduces the time it takes me to understand their style. Otherwise, it could take weeks or months for me to get to know them and their behavior style. By doing a communication behavior profile, in 20 minutes I know more than I could ever imagine about them.

The profile is quite amazing. The client answers 24 questions and based on the individual's responses, a personalized analysis report is generated detailing general characteristics of their style, guidelines for what to do and not to do when communicating with you, tips for communicating with each Behavior Style (DISC), how others might perceive Keys to Motivating and Managing you, and so on.

For our purposes, it is not necessary that you do a complete behavior work-up in order to use the DISC approach. If you are interested in learning more about DISC, visit my website.

Instead of using the comprehensive DISC assessment here, we will simplify things. Since the DISC approach focused on observable behavior, you can identify a person's primary behavior style by just looking at two continuums from Dr. Marston's book. The first continuum details Passive (Introverted) and Active (Extroverted) factors, and the second details Task-Oriented and People-Oriented factors.

Four Behavioral Factors

There is no right or wrong behavioral factor; each of us has various degrees of each. When I do a complete profile, it shows a graph depicting your ranking in each of the four quadrants. You can rank high or low in each one. So in a complete profile, you will see a combination of all four traits with one style being your highest. For the sake of clarity, we are going to focus on the highest-ranking style.

As I describe the different continua on the next few pages, try to place yourself (and/or the Receiver) on the continuum graph below and determine what style you are.

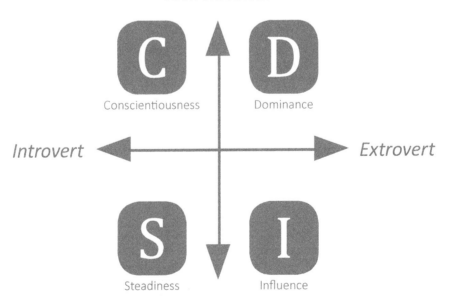

Task Receiver

C Conscientiousness

D Dominance

Introvert ← → *Extrovert*

S Steadiness

I Influence

Feeling Receiver

Warning

This by no means makes you a communication behavioral expert. So do not apply it that way. Please do not finish this chapter and start diagnosing your friends, co-workers, spouse, or in-laws. I am giving you just enough information to be dangerous.

I know that people are complex. At times it may appear I am stereotyping. In a way, I am, in order to help you start to see the differences. Remember these are guidelines to help you become more aware of the differences that may exist between you and the Receiver. Once you are more aware, then you can begin adapting.

Also, note that this process is done silently. It really does not help to tell someone that he or she is a Dominant or Influencer style communicator. This is a silent language to be used by you to help you plan and deliver your message.

Introvert vs. Extrovert

When having an interpersonal conversation, DISC will help you indentify whether the Receiver is an introvert or extrovert, so that you can customize your communication. When we look at introverts vs. extroverts, we are looking at two areas: personality style, and the way the Person processes information.

How Do You Identify Introverts?

We all know someone who we would label as an introvert. If you went to a party, they could be the person who:

- Stands in the corner at a party, in a smaller group, and is listening.

- Is quieter and speaks with more of a monotone in a conversation.

- Shows little or no emotion and you are not sure what they are thinking.

- Keeps their distance when you are having a conversation.

- Does not use many gestures or hand movements.

- Talks slowly and/or quietly with less energy.

How Introverts Process Information

The second way to identify an introvert has to do with how they process information. Introverts tend to think before they speak. They process information internally. Therefore, when you meet someone and you ask him/her a question, and he/she takes a while to respond, this may mean that he/she is an introvert or possibly a task-oriented person (which I will cover a little later in this chapter). Introverts do not normally respond quickly to a question and that is because they are filtering the information that they want to share to make sure that they say it correctly or say it in a way that won't hurt others' feelings.

Knowing as much as you can about the introvert will help you when crafting your message and building a relationship.

How to Interact with Introverts

- Ask open-ended questions to draw out the person's thoughts.
- Go relatively slow and be patient.
- Give them time to think.
- Don't come on too strong.
- Earn their trust in small steps.
- Allow plenty of time for decision-making.
- Minimize the expression of emotion.
- Reduce risk—offer testimonials, or a trial period.

How Do You Identify Extroverts?

We all know someone whom we would label as an extrovert. If you went to a party, they could be the person who:

- Is talking and seems to be the center of attention.
- Speaks loudly and with vocal variety in a conversation.
- Shows more energy/emotion.
- Makes eye contact.
- Uses different facial expressions.
- Is a little too close and you can tell what they had for dinner on their breath.
- Is moving his or her hands so wildly they knock the other person's drink out of his or her hands.
- Is talking very quickly and you almost have a hard time understanding what they are saying.

How Extroverts Process Information

The second way to identify an extrovert has to do with how they process information. Extroverts often speak before they think things through. They process information externally.

They tend to exhibit signs of Logorrhea, which I like to call "verbal diarrhea." They sometimes get themselves into trouble because they don't have a filter that is working. They tend to process information externally and often use a sounding board to help them think through the issue.

At the beginning of a conversation, they may ramble or process information aloud. What they say may not be what they eventually mean to say.

How to Interact with Extroverts

- Plan a little extra time for the conversations because they need to talk.

- Listen patiently and ask close-ended questions to guide the conversation and help them get to the point quicker.

- Do not try to control the conversation—try to guide it.

- Bring some energy to the conversation (especially if you are an introvert).

- Do not be afraid to speak up.

- Make friendly eye contact.

- Show appreciation and enthusiasm for ideas.

Task vs. Feeling

The other continuum is more difficult to read at first glance. That is why I suggest if you meet someone you do not know that well, try to determine if they are an introvert or an extrovert. These two areas are easier to read because they are based on observable behaviors.

The other continuum, task versus feeling, takes a little longer to learn how to read. The following is a brief overview of these two components.

INTENTION

MESSAGE

PERSON

ACTIVATE

CLARITY

TRANSFORM

How Do You Identify Task Receivers?

- More task-focused.
- Tend to keep feelings guarded (formal).
- More organized.
- More precise about the use of time (early or on time for meetings).
- Asks detailed questions.
- Focuses on facts and details.

How Do You Interact with Task Receivers?

- Make sure you are well prepared.
- Have plenty of facts and figures (seeing is believing).
- Be prepared for skepticism.
- Answer all of their questions.
- Be efficient and businesslike.
- Don't get too close to them.
- Avoid criticizing or judging ideas.
- Do not try to build personal relationships too quickly.

How Do You Identify Feeling Receivers?

- More relational-oriented.
- Tends to show emotion (informal).
- Less organized.
- Imprecise about the use of time (can be late for meetings).
- Focuses on opinions/stories.

How Do You Interact with Feeling Receivers?

- If possible, let them "experience" what you are communicating.
- Don't drive on facts and figures.
- Talk in terms of people and stories.
- Use many examples.
- Adjust your approach, don't come on too strong.
- Provide plenty of reassurance.
- Ask about their family, children, etc. Be prepared to talk about yours.
- Let the person know you like them and appreciate them.
- Be aware that this person may have a hard time saying "NO" and may be easily persuaded.

Remember the four styles:

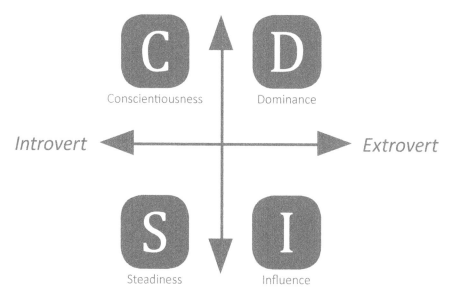

PERSON

DISC Exercises

You can communicate effectively by adapting your style to meet the needs of the receiver's style. Here are four people who have different communication styles. See how well you comprehend this concept by identifying which of the four styles we discussed over the previous pages.

Now read each paragraph and answer the questions after each. Feel free to refer back to previous sections for guidance. I will give you the correct DISC styles for each person at the end of the exercises. Good luck!

1. Marion

You have just been informed of some changes that will be taking place in the immediate future and you need to communicate these changes with Marion. Marion is a very patient person, yet somewhat reserved. She uses an unemotional tone when conversing with people and is easygoing. Usually you cannot tell whether she agrees or disagrees with your ideas.

What DISC style is Marion and why?

_____

_____

_____

How would you approach Marion regarding communicating these changes?

_____

_____

_____

2. John

John is always in a hurry. You need to talk with him about an important issue. You catch him on the run and begin to tell him. He abruptly interrupts you and asks you to get to the point. You feel a little intimidated.

What DISC style is John and why?

_____

_____

_____

What is the best way to continue your conversation with John?

_____

_____

_____

3. Mary

You and Mary are working together on a project. Whenever you meet with Mary, it always takes longer than you think. Mary likes to update you on work and her personal life. She can sometimes be imprecise about the use of time. During today's meeting, you mentioned to her that the project completion date is only six weeks away, to which she replied, "We have plenty of time."

What DISC style is Mary and why?

_____

_____

_____

What can you do to improve the effectiveness of the meeting with Mary?

_____

_____

_____

4. James

You and James are working on a project together. You are supposed to meet at 10:00 a.m. You arrive at 10:03 and James looks at his watch. You begin to tell him what you have done so far on the project. James listens, but does not look enthusiastic. When you have finished talking, James proceeds to ask you some very specific questions about costs and deadlines. Then James says, "Do you think this is really the right thing to do?"

What DISC style is James and why?

_____

_____

_____

How can you adjust your style to continue the meeting?

_____

_____

_____

What DISC Style Are You?

In my "Lead with STYLE" workshop, I discuss that, in order to be a more effective communicator and leader, you need to blend your DISC style with the DISC style of the Receiver. In addition, I talk about the value of knowing your own style, maximizing your strengths, and improving your weaknesses.

Look again at the diagram below and try to identify your DISC style.

You can do this by answering the following two questions:

1. Are you an introvert or extrovert?

2. Are you task or feeling oriented?

Now that you have a good guess as to your style, look at the areas for improvement below and see how you can improve your communication.

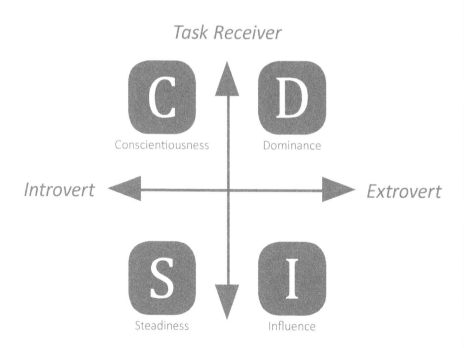

Answers to DISC Exercises

Let us see how well you can read others and identify the four styles. Here are their correct DISC styles:

1. Marion is an S-Steady 2. John is a D-Dominant 3. Mary is an I-Influencer 4. James is a C- Compliant

How You Can Improve Your DISC Style

DISC Areas for Improvement

If you are a Dominant Style, try to:

- Learn to listen better

- Be less controlling

- Focus more on relationships

- Take time to explain why

- Have more empathy

If you are an Influencer Style, try to:

- Talk less, listen more

- Focus on details/facts

- Slow down

- Be less impulsive

- Follow through

If you are a Steady Style, try to:

- Be more open to change

- Be more direct

- Face confrontation

- Initiate more, be proactive

- Increase your pace in achieving results

If you are a Conscientious Style, try to:

- Be more decisive

- Focus more on people /relationships (vs. facts)

- Be open to other's ideas

- Join the team in taking risks

- Focus on what's right (vs. what's wrong)

What Gets in the Way?

In addition to personality styles, we also need to anticipate other personal differences that will get in the way of us communicating with IMPACT. If we become more aware of the communication differences, remove them, or adapt to work around them, we can begin to build deeper relationships and improve the reception of our Message.

The following are eight examples of personal differences that can get in the way of communicating with IMPACT.

1. Education and Experience

Our education and experience, or that of others, can sometimes be a barrier in communicating with IMPACT.

For example, I was talking with a group of attorneys and as part of my preparation for this presentation, I interviewed a few potential attendees, a senior partner, a junior partner, and a new lawyer who had just passed the bar. I asked each of them a series of questions to tailor my Business Attraction Factor workshop.

As I talked with Mary, the new lawyer, she made a comment that I found insightful. We were talking about how much competition is out there when she said, "Being good is no longer good enough. There are a lot of good lawyers out there."

I opened the workshop with her quote on a slide: "Being good is no longer good enough!"

I did not tell the group who I was quoting and proceeded to ask the lawyers, "Who said this?"

They began responding with the names of many famous lawyers: Clarence Darrow, F. Lee Bailey, Gladys Root, Thurgood Marshall, Janet Reno, Johnnie Cochran, and so forth.

Then I finally told them, "None of you are correct, the person who said that is in our room today and she is sitting over there…. Mary."

The group was shocked. They could not believe a new, inexperienced, wet-behind-the-ears lawyer could have said that. Many times, we can either give too much or too little credit to the receiver based on their experience or education and this will affect how we communicate with them.

2. Status

Have you ever found yourself changing how you communicate based on the status of the Receiver?

Many of us have been raised to respect a person's position or status. President, doctor, police officer, priest, rabbi, minister, teacher, spouse, parent, boss…. All of these and many other titles or positions may have an influence on how you communicate with a Receiver.

At the same time, remember that your position and status could influence how someone might communicate with you. An employee might screen what they tell you based on your position in the organization, not because of you as a person, but because of the role you play.

3. Language

Today, many workplaces are multicultural, and so we have language differences as well. However, you can have language barriers even within that same language.

I remember my first trip to New York City. One hot afternoon, we stopped in a store to get some ice cream to cool off.

I thought a nice refreshing ice cream soda would do the trick. So I said to the clerk, "I would like a soda - a cola with vanilla ice cream."

She replied, "You mean a float."

I answered, "No, I mean a soda."

She said, "A soda is plain and a float has ice cream."

I said, "A float is in a parade, and I want a soda."

Even two people speaking the same language can have a language barrier. Keep in mind that certain regions of a country use different words to describe the same thing. For example, in the U.S., people use various names for a sub sandwich. Some regions call it a "hero," others a "hoagie," "grinder," "Italian," and even a "torpedo."

This is also true for different generations. I did some volunteer work as a "big brother" back in the late 80s and one young man told me that he would like me to come see his "crib" sometime.

My first thought was, this poor kid, he is fifteen and still sleeps in a crib. I did not realize that he was using this name to refer to the place where he lived.

4. Health

Did you ever notice that when you don't feel well, are sleep-deprived, or under stress, you are not as good a communicator? When we don't feel well, we may take comments more personally, have a shorter attention span, and be impatient.

Think about how personal health barriers are going to affect your communication and that of the Receiver.

5. Stereotyping

People often make assumptions about others when they communicate to them based on how they look, act, or sound.

My wife and I were on a flight to Europe one time when there came an announcement over the plane's intercom: "If there is a doctor on the plane, please come to aisle 12."

My wife was sleeping, so I woke her and told her they called for a doctor to report to aisle 12. She went there to see if she could help.

When Beth arrived, one of the men there, seeing that she was a woman, assumed she was a nurse and told her, "We don't need a nurse. We already have a doctor. Thanks for coming, though."

This happened to us in the 1990s, not in the 1940s. Stereotypes still exist to this day and we need to be mindful of them when we communicate with any kind of Receiver.

Another example is when I was in Japan trying to speak with the locals. Some of the Japanese people I met spoke a little English and they would want me to communicate with them in English, even though there was an interpreter there to help me. Well, when I tried to speak with them in English, I found myself dong something unusual. For some odd reason I thought if I just talked louder, they would understand me better. So in a loud voice I would say, "Good morning. How are you?"

They would respond with a little English, "Fine, thank you," and then quickly start talking in Japanese. Of course, I did not know what they were saying so my interpreter would eventually tell me what they said. This is when I realized I was talking louder because the interpreter told me they said: "Please stop shouting, I am not deaf."

6. Fear

Fear can inhibit our communication. Depending on your personality style and your experience with the personality style of the Receiver, you might let the fear of the result from the communication hinder the communication.

For example, when preparing to communicate with a Dominant style person, you might be apprehensive about the way they might respond to your conversation. Dominant Receivers can, at times, be impatient. In addition, if you have had prior experience with this Receiver, you might let the way they treated you in the past interfere with you having a present conversation.

On the other hand, if you have to make a presentation or speech to a group, your anxiety about speaking in public might inhibit you from taking on speaking opportunities. In fact, studies show that speaking in public is a common fear.

So what do you do? Not communicate with others? Of course not. You take a few moments to explore and adjust your perception of the fear.

Years ago, I heard some say that the word "fear" is an acronym, standing for Fantasized Experience Appearing Real. Therefore, when we are faced with fear as a roadblock to communication, the best place to start is to check out the fear. Is it real or imaginary?

The following questions might help you uncover what you are worried about. Work through this to move forward:

- What worries you the most about having this conversation?

- What do you fear might happen? How much of this is real?

- What is the worst thing that could happen?

- What could happen if I do not have the conversation?

- What can you do to reduce your anxiety about having this conversation?

We all have some fears when it comes to communicating. However, if we take the time to think it through, be proactive, and practice, we can reduce the fear and increase the comfort level to approach the communication situation from a more realistic perspective.

7. Generations

Do you take into consideration that when the Receiver was born influences your communication with them?

Here are the four main categories for the various generations.

- Members of the Silent Generation (also known as Traditionalists) were born before 1946.

- Baby Boomers were born between 1946 and 1964.

- Members of Gen-X were born between 1965 and 1980.

- Millennials (sometimes called Gen Y or Generation Next) were born after 1981.

Each generation is influenced by the main events that occurred during their time frame. Keep this in mind as you are communicating.

8. Attention Span

We each have different levels of attention span. Some of us have short attention spans and others have longer attention spans. Which one do you have?

In reality, we each possess both. It all depends on the topic and the person.

If any conversation moves toward golf, I have a short attention span. I really cannot comprehend the game and do not see how someone can spend hours watching people on television hit a ball with a stick.

On the other hand, if the conversation is about Italian food, then I have a long attention span. I love to talk about food, especially Italian food. All four of my grandparents came from Italy and food was so important in my upbringing. For example, we plan what we want to eat for lunch while eating breakfast. We all do this, and if we are speaking with a person we like to be around, we will have a longer attention span than when we speak to someone who annoys us.

Give some thought to what your attention span might be versus what it needs to be, and then plan accordingly.

INTENTION

MESSAGE

PERSON

ACTIVATE

CLARITY

TRANSFORM

IMPACT Insight: Attention Span

Pay attention to your shifting attention span. Here are a few questions that will help.

Shorter Attention Span:

1. For what topics do I have a short attention span?

2. With which people do I have a short attention span?

3. How will I adapt to overcome my shorter attention span with this Receiver?

Longer Attention Span:

1. For what topics do I have a long attention span?

2. With which people do I have a long attention span?

3. How will I adapt to overcome my longer attention span with this Receiver?

Individual and Group Differences

In the following sections, we will go over the different ways to communicate with both individual and group Receivers. A group receiver refers to multiple people or an audience.

Individual Receiver

Working with many senior executives, I have found that certain people respond better to one mode of communication over another.

As we discussed in the Message chapter, people have certain communication method preferences. The better you tailor the Message to the Receiver, the better the Receiver will understand. This means not only tailoring to their personality but also to their method preference.

I called a CEO recently and his voicemail outlined his priority for handling correspondence: "The best way to reach me is in this order: email, then phone, then regular mail." I really liked knowing his preference and did exactly as he asked.

Keep in mind that not everyone has the same preference. Several things can drive it. Here are a few issues that might drive the Receiver's preferences:

Skill Level — If you are not a great typist, you may prefer a phone call to an email.

Personality Style – Introverts may prefer email and texting over face-to-face or a phone call.

The Issue – If you want to have documentation of your communication, you may prefer email, or if you do not want a trail, you might prefer a phone call. My preference is phone for complicated communication and email for simpler communication.

Generation – Younger generations are more accustomed to texting, emailing, and social media.

Privacy – Some people do not give out their cell phone number because they like a certain level of privacy. For others, the only number they respond to is their cell number.

Preference - Communicate with Receivers according to their communication preference. Years ago, I heard someone say, "If they are a reader, you write to them; if they are a listener, you tell them."

> *"If there is any one secret of success, it lies in the ability to get the other person's point of view and see things from that person's angle as well as from your own."*
>
> — *Henry Ford*

Group Receivers

It is not as easy to use the DISC process when trying to understand a group of people, yet you want to find out as much as possible about the Group Receiver.

I talk about the importance of analyzing the audience in my presentation skills and media training workshops.

In advance of the event, I recommend doing research and finding out as much as possible about an audience before you speak. I have an Audience Analysis Form (AAF) with a series of questions I use to gather information. In addition, I like to get to the event early and walk around meeting attendees and asking them questions regarding why they are here. All this helps you get to learn more about the audience so you can tailor your remarks to the group and build rapport.

Using the HW5 method discussed in the Message chapter is a great tool to help you analyze your audience before you deliver a presentation.

Group Presentation Customization in Action

I was asked to speak to a large asphalt company on the topic of "Leading and Communicating with Style." Over the afternoon of the workshop, I taught the four communication styles (DISC), discussing the value of identifying and adapting your leadership and communication styles to the styles of your employees.

From my audience analysis and research, I discovered that many of the leaders had been promoted internally into their leadership role within their company. Some were former truck drivers, and most supervised truck drivers and office staff. Therefore, I wanted to find a way to connect with them.

It just so happened that during my summer and winter college breaks, I worked for my hometown city street department. We plowed snow in the winter and patched asphalt in the summer. We were divided up into truck crews each morning, and would go out with a driver. Over the time I worked there, I rotated crews and had the chance to work with many different truck drivers.

After a great deal of forethought, when it came time to customize my presentation to an asphalt company audience many years later, I used the different drivers (Joey, Chucky, Teddy, and Butch) from my college job to demonstrate the four different communication styles:

D – Fast-paced and bottom-line (Joey)

I – Talkative and enthusiastic (Chucky)

S - Friendly and supportive (Teddy)

C – Careful and analytical (Butch)

My stories and personal anecdotes about these gentlemen made the material more relevant to the audience and helped them better understand their styles.

Whenever possible, I try to find ways to tie my content into the interest and experiences of my audience. My secret is spending time upfront to research my audience and tap into my own experiences whenever possible to customize my presentation.

Anticipate and Deal with Different Styles

Here is another example about doing your audience analysis in advance. Mary had been around in her firm for 25 years and was not excited to come to my communication skills workshop. In fact, the meeting planner told me that she would be difficult, and that I should not pay attention to her body language because she would be sure to let me know that she was not happy to be there. I was so glad that the planner prepared me because, when Mary entered the room, I knew immediately who she was. From her closed posture to her strained facial expressions, it was clear she was not happy to be there.

I like to mingle with the people in the room before a workshop, so I stopped over to say hello to Mary. You could feel the chill in the air as I got close to her. She said hello back, and that was about it.

It got worse: at one point during the workshop, I could hear Mary making groaning sounds. I looked over and caught a glimpse of her expression. It was frightening. That was when I put my plan into action.

Most presenters in my situation would have ignored her because they would not want to engage her. Not me. I wanted to prove to the meeting planner that I, the communication expert, could walk my talk. I realized that the issue I had raised frustrated her, so I called on her.

With confidence, I said, "Mary, I know you have been working in this department for a few years–how many, exactly?"

"Twenty-five," she barked back.

"Tell me, Mary, how has the department changed in terms of the way customers treat staff?"

Surprisingly, she responded candidly by saying, "I am so glad you asked." Then she went into a five-minute history lesson. It was very interesting and informative, even though she presented it with anger and frustration.

When Mary finished speaking, I thanked her, and summarized her findings for the group. Then I transitioned back to the agenda by complimenting her, "Well, Mary, you hit the nail on the head. You see, what Mary shared is exactly why we are here today...."

As soon as I finished that statement, you could see a shift in Mary's demeanor. She reminded me of the Grinch, from Dr. Seuss' *How the Grinch Stole Christmas*, when his heart grows at the end. She grew a smile and began to sit up straight.

After the program, while I was talking with the meeting planner, Mary came up to me and said with a smile, "Thank you for the program. This was one of the best I've attended in a while." Of course, the meeting planner just looked at me in awe. I could not have been happier. So, what did I do right? I used the IMPACT process.

INTENTION

MESSAGE

PERSON

ACTIVATE

CLARIFY

TRANSFORM

Using the IMPACT Process

As a way to show you the complete IMPACT process in action, let's walk through how I handled Mary using all six principles.

Planning - IMP

Once I identified the Person (Mary), I walked through the IMP planning process and came up with a game plan.

Intention - First, I identified my Intention, which was to make Mary feel appreciated.

Message - Next I thought through the message, how to let Mary know that her opinion mattered.

Person - Finally, I worked on this principle, knowing in advance that Mary's personality and attitude might be a barrier to my effectively communication with her.

Action - ACT

Let me introduce the three keys to ACT process in this next section as I continue to share how I used these three keys to address the Mary situation:

Activate - By asking Mary a few questions, I activated and engaged her in the communication.

Clarify – Mary's response to my questions was fairly long (five minutes). By summarizing Mary's points and tying them back to the topic of the workshop, I was able bring clarity to Mary and help her see the value she brings to the group.

Transform – As a result of following the previous five principles, my interaction with Mary helped transform her attitude and demeanor.

Using the IMPACT Process to plan and implement a conversation can minimize the risks of communicating with a difficult person. And in the case of Mary, it made all the difference.

"Nothing in life is more important than the ability to communicate effectively."

— *Gerald Ford*

SUMMARY - Person

The last step on the planning stage (IMP) is the P - Person. In order to fulfill your Intention, you want to craft your Message to match the needs of your Receiver, the Person.

Not all Receivers are created equal. So keep in mind the personality/communication styles we discussed in the chapter. The better you know the Receiver, the better you can achieve your intention.

In the next principle, Activate, we will talk more about bringing the message to life to keep both you and the Receiver engaged in the communication.

> *"The meeting of two personalities is like the contact of two chemical substances: if there is any reaction, both are transformed."*
>
> — *Carl Jung*

IMPACT Insight (Person)

Here are a few insights from this chapter. Which ones do you want to focus on this week? Be flexible. Whenever you can, adapt and blend your communication style to the Receiver's style.

Practice the "The Platinum Rule®" which states: "Do unto others as they want done unto them." Remember:

Introverts process information internally (they tend to think before they speak).

Extroverts process information externally (they tend to speak before they think).

Task oriented Receivers tend to prefer more data and details.

Feelings oriented Receivers tend to prefer stories/examples. Let them experience the message.

Be aware of the communication differences (experience, status, stereotyping, attention span, and so on) and remove them, and/or adapt to work around them.

Use the information you learned about the Person (whether it be an individual Receiver or a group) and tailor your message to their needs by practicing the "The Platinum Rule.®"

IMPACT Reflection (Person)

"What is my behavior style (DISC)? Am I an Introvert or Extrovert? Task or Feeling?"

"How will my style impact my communication with the Receiver?"

"Based on my behavior style (DISC), what are some areas I want to work on to be a better communicator?"

"Do I know the behavior style (DISC) of my Receiver: Are they an Introvert or Extrovert? Task or Feeling?"

"How will I blend my behavior style to that of the Receiver to improve the communication?"

"Which Receiver behavior style(s) (DISC) is more difficult for me to communicate with?"

"Which of the eight communication differences might get in the way of having effective communication?"

"How will I manage or deal with these eight communication differences?"

"When communicating with a group, do I use the HW5 method to learn more about the Receivers?"

IMPACT Application (Person)

Below are lists of various situations where you may want to apply the Person principle in your daily routine. Pick one or two that are applicable to you and list a person, situation, and time when you would want to apply this principle.

Presentation (examples: Staff meeting, committee update, board report, training seminar, speech, etc.)

Person: _____

Situation: _____

Date to Apply Principle: _____

Interpersonal Communication (examples: Conversation, phone call, luncheon, etc.)

Person: _____

Situation: _____

Date to Apply Principle: _____

Marketing/Sales Communication (examples: Sales call, luncheon, presentation, etc.)

Person: _____

Situation: _____

Date to Apply Principle: _____

Public Communication (examples: Social media, radio/television interviews, video conferences, etc.)

Person: _____

Situation: _____

Date to Apply Principle: _____

INTENTION

MESSAGE

PERSON

ACTIVATE

CLARIFY

TRANSFORM

PHASE 2
THE ACTION PHASE (ACT)

A   Activate

C   Clarify

T   Transform

Activate (ak'tiv ate) – verb

causing action, motion, or change that is acting, functioning, working, moving, etc.

to affect mentally, physically, and/or emotionally in a way that moves the receiver toward an intended result

PRINCIPLE 4
Activate

- What is an Active Communicator?
- Three Components of Active Communication
- Four Mindsets that Drive Communication
- Forms of Communication – Benefits & Challenges
- Difference Between Listening and Hearing
- Your Questions Drive the Conversation
- Mentally Engage in the Communication (Active Mind)
- Activate Your Group Communication
- 18 Tips for Improving Your Slides
- IMPACT Insight
- IMPACT Reflection
- IMPACT Application

INTENTION

MESSAGE

PERSON

ACTIVATE

CLARIFY

TRANSFORM

PRINCIPLE 4

Activate

"Activate your Message by making sure you and the Receiver are physically, mentally, and emotionally engaged in the communication."

A is for Activate

How will you engage the Receiver? Most people have shorter attention spans these days. In order to keep their attention, we need to get the Receiver involved physically, mentally, and emotionally.

Once you have crafted the Message based on your Intention and taken into consideration how you will adapt the message to the Person, it is time to focus on how you will Activate the message to keep both you, the Sender, and the Receiver engaging and participating in the communication process.

Do You Proactively Think About How to Engage the Receiver in the Communication?

One of my Fortune 500 company clients asked me to help turn ten of their managers into coaches. One such sales manager, named Judy, was having a difficult time dealing with an internal sales person named John, who tended to be aggressive and defensive. In her coaching sessions with him, John would always end up taking charge.

In my coaching sessions with Judy, I explored this situation further by activating the conversation and engaging her in the solution with questions.

"What does John remind you of?" I asked.

"A grizzly bear," Judy responded.

"What would you do if you were trying to deal with a grizzly bear?" I questioned.

"Give him food and turn and run in the other direction," she said, with a smile.

After a few more minutes of questioning, Judy uncovered her plan. Whenever John would start to take control of the session (like a bear attacking), she would respond by acknowledging or thanking him for his input, (throwing the bear food) and start asking questions (changing direction).

I spoke with Judy a few weeks later. Guess what? She just had the best session ever with John. By thinking of the grizzly bear metaphor, she was able to keep John on track and get the meeting done in record time, while not feeling attacked.

Seek and Ye Shall Find

One way to activate the Receiver is to ask questions. Through my early years as a talk show host, my thirty years as an entrepreneur, and my practical experience as a business coach, I have had a great deal of practice in asking questions.

What if instead of being an active communicator with Judy, I had simply told her what to do (linear communication). Would she have had such a quick result? I doubt it.

Instead of telling Judy what to do, I activated the communication by using questions to help her come up with the answer. By asking Judy some questions, she realized she needed the metaphor to help her deal more effectively with John. Not only did it help Judy stay focused, it actually made her session with John more fun. Compare that to her prior meetings where she was feeling anxious and uncomfortable due to John's controlling nature.

That is the beauty of being an active communicator. You can make a good employee better or help someone develop skills to increase performance all on his or her own by actively engaging them in the conversation.

What is an Active Communicator?

- Realizes that non-verbal communication is an important part of the message.

- Understands the emotion in the message.
- Is aware of what's going on during the communication.
- Uses a variety of tools and techniques to communicate the message.

Three Components of Active Communication

There are three components to Active Communication:

1. Thinking (Active Mind)
2. Articulating (Active Voice, Heart, and Body)
3. Listening (Active Ears and Eyes)

1. Thinking (Active Mind)

Communication starts in the thinking phase whether you consciously are aware of it or not. Your thinking or mindset drives your behavior and your behavior (the way we communicate) drives the results we get.

Not only do you want to identify the Intention, it is also important that you actively get in the right mindset. What you are thinking affects how you feel and how you feel affects how you communicate.

When you change your Intention, you change how you listen and respond. For example, let's say you are having lunch with a prospective client. If your intention is to make a connection with the Receiver, you will act differently than if you go into the luncheon with the mindset that you are going to close the deal.

The following are four mindsets that can drive the way you Activate the Message and influence your communication and listening ability.

A. Adult Mindset

In his book, *Games People Play*, Dr. Eric Berne discussed three modes of behavior, referred to as Transactional Analysis (TA).

The three behavior modes are:

1. Child Mode

2. Parent Mode

3. Adult Mode

The mode you are in influences how you see the world, what you hear, and how you respond.

When in Child Mode, you act emotionally. Anger and despair dominate reason, similarly to how a child might respond.

When in Parent Mode, you act controlling, and judgment dominates reason (as a strict parent might). If others are not doing it the "right way," you will respond by telling them so.

The best mode to be in is the Adult Mode. In the Adult Mode, you focus on the facts, the situation, or the behavior, and not the person. You are neutral and open to listening without the biases of the other two modes. You refrain from judgment until after you have listened and gathered more information.

> *"If we want a love message to be heard,*
> *it has got to be sent out. To keep a lamp burning,*
> *we have to keep putting oil in it."*
>
> — *Mother Teresa*

B. Loving-Truth Mindset

One of the ways I get into a good mindset is to spend a few moments in the morning getting ready for the day. I find if I start out with a positive mindset, it is easier to stay there.

Years ago, I read a short story in one of my morning meditative booklets that stuck with me. It was entitled "Loving Truth." The overall message was that when you are going to give others feedback, you should come from a place of caring and love for the Receiver.

Our mindset drives our behavior. It is easy to forget why (Intention) we are giving the feedback. If I come from a place of frustration, anger, impatience, or judgment (Child Mode or Parent Mode), this will manifest itself into my Message. I try to remember to communicate from a place of caring (using the Adult Mode) and share my Message in the form of loving-truth.

Just as I started my day by getting mentally ready, you should do the same before you communicate with the Receiver. Take a few minutes to determine what your current mindset is and what you want your mindset to be, and then communicate from this mindset.

C. Family Mindset

My dad had a favorite saying, "Treat me good, I'll treat you better!"

My dad's philosophy has always stuck with me. Both my parents and my Italian grandparents taught me the importance of family. I also had numerous aunts, uncles, and cousins within minutes from where I lived. From all of them, I learned the values of treating everyone like family.

If my dad hired you to fix something at the house that he couldn't fix himself and you treated him fairly, not only would he pay you, he would also give you a gift (maybe some ripe tomatoes or fresh green peppers from his garden or a bottle of wine). Therefore, I try to apply this same "treat you better" principle to my interactions with others.

When I was getting my Master's degree at Ohio University, I worked as the graduate director of an all-male upper class residence hall. I had a student staff that reported to me and together we tried to keep the young students on the right path. This was my first official leadership role and I did my best to follow what I learned from my family and treated my staff and student residents as family.

I built some great relationships with my staff and students at Ohio University. Even to this day, a group of my former student staff and residents get together every New Year's Eve with our families to ring in the New Year. My kids would not miss this even if you paid them.

You do not have to be of Italian descent to treat people like family. This is a simple mindset that you can adopt.

How would you treat co-workers or employees if they were family?

D. Customer Mindset - Treat Everyone Like a Customer

One day, when I came home from a full day meeting with a client, I was exhausted. All I wanted to do was go upstairs, get out of my suit, and relax.

As soon I walked in the door, my young son had a series of questions for me. I could sense myself starting to get frustrated, and then it happened. I lashed out with, "Can I just go get changed?"

Since I had never responded this way before, he was blind-sided. I could see the look on his face; he had no idea that I was going to explode. Has something like this ever happened to you?

How would you treat family (or co-workers) if they were customers?

I realized that day that if I am not careful, I might treat my customers better than I treat my immediate family. If a customer had bombarded me with questions, I would have responded differently.

The way I see it, everyone we interact with are our customers. I put people into two categories: external customers, those who buy products and services from us, and internal customers, those who we interact with on a daily basis: co-workers, family, and friends.

If we are not careful, we might treat the external customer better than we treat our internal customers. By thinking of co-workers, family, and friends as internal customers, and staying in the adult state of mind when you are communicating with them, we can increase our chances of treating them with the respect and love they deserve.

"They may forget what you said, but they will never forget how you made them feel."

— *Carl W. Buechner*

Your Mindset Drives Behavior

The right mindset is critical, especially when communicating with others. The above four mindsets are examples of how your mindset drives the way you respond. Spend a few minutes identifying and adjusting your mindset before you communicate with the Receiver.

2. Articulating (Active Voice, Heart, and Body)

What you are thinking affects how you feel, and how you feel affects how you communicate. Now that you are actively in a good mindset, it is time to articulate the message.

How will you put your thoughts into words, using as many of the senses as possible to communicate with the Receiver?

Communicate in 3-D

My family and I went to see the 3-D movie Avatar on an IMAX screen. With all the hype, we thought there was no way it could be that good. We have seen many 3-D movies before and they had always seemed fake. However, when we left the theater, we were all impressed. It felt like you were right there. There were times when we physically moved in our seats to avoid being hit by a character. There were times that we were mentally problem solving alongside the hero. There were even times when we could feel the emotion, excitement, and adventure as if we were the characters themselves. As you can gather, the film made an impact on us.

Wouldn't it be great if we could communicate in 3-D? I mean, wouldn't you like to have people experience your message physically, mentally, and emotionally?

Guess what? You can.

How we articulate or communicate the message is much more than talking.

Forms of Communication

Communicate in 3-D. Incorporate the three dimensions of your message. You can articulate or communicate your Message in three general ways: with our spoken words, written words, and non-verbally.

In the following pages, we will discuss the benefits and challenges of each form of communication:

1. Spoken

2. Non-verbal

3. Written

Spoken Word *Active Voice*	Non-verbal *Active Body*	Written Word *Active Words*
Face-to-face	Facial expressions	Lettter
Phone call	Eye contact	Email
Speech	Gestures	Text
Presentation	Posture	Social media
	Movement	

Spoken Communications

The spoken word is primarily articulated through your voice. This category includes face-to-face conversations, phone calls, presentations, and speeches to groups.

Benefits:

- Personal.

- Allows for immediate clarification/feedback.

- Flexible—the final message is co-created.

- Good for communication that requires discussion or agreement.

- Message is influenced by voice, tone, and non-verbal behavior.

- More immediate response than written (when connected with the person).

- You can see and hear the person's non-verbal gestures.

- You can tell if the other person is engaged in the communication and adjust accordingly if they are not.

Challenges:

- Delivery can have a big influence on the message.

- Message is influenced by voice, tone, and non-verbal behavior.

- Tends to be a longer communication than written.

- It is not permanent. So there is no written record to refer back to for clarification.

- Distractions may interfere with the reception of the message.

Non-Verbal Communication

Non-verbal communication is primarily articulated through your body. This category includes: facial expressions, eye contact, gestures, posture, and movement.

INTENTION

MESSAGE

PERSON

ACTIVATE

CLARIFY

TRANSFORM

Benefits:

- Reinforce the message.

- Add meaning to the Message through voice, tone, and non-verbal behavior.

- Can tell if the other person is engaged in the communication and adjust accordingly if they are not.

- Can show emotion.

- Can show signs of conflict or confusion that can give you a clue to check to see if there is an issue.

Challenges:

- Can be misinterpreted.

- Message is influenced by voice, tone, and non-verbal-behavior.

- Non-verbal can contradict the words.

- Can be distracting.

- Can lead you into a false sense of security.

Written Communication

Written communication is primarily articulated through your words. This category includes letters, emails, texts, and social media.

Benefits:

- Good for complicated communication—when giving people directions or instructions.

- Decrease chances of miscommunication.

- Permanent and can be referred back to for details.

- More concise.

- Can read (or send) the message at your convenience.

- Can reach others no matter where they are (example: text message).

- Have time to think and rewrite before finally sending the message.

- Good for linear (one-way) communication that requires little discussion.

Challenges:

- Impersonal and is not a good way to build rapport or deepen the relationship.

- Can't transfer emotion as well.

- Linear in nature and can be misinterpreted. No one is there to clarify any misunderstandings.

- No immediate feedback.

- Cannot easily see or interrupt the emotion behind the message.

- Electronic written communication (email, text) is a fast and convenient way to communicate because people feel the need to write and respond quickly, which can lead to errors and incomplete messages.

- Can make a difficult situation worse because people selectively perceive what the message means based on their beliefs and experience.

- Easier to hide behind and avoid conflict.

> *"The most important thing in communication is to listen to what is not being said."*
>
> — *Peter Drucker*

3. Listening (Active Ears, Eyes, and Heart)

Listen actively with your eyes (for non-verbal), ears (for words), and heart (for emotions). Active listening is "real" listening. Active listening requires patience, practice, presence, and persistence.

Passive listening is more common in today's world, both at work and at home. That is because passive listening is easier and the center of focus is more on you than the talker.

Ask questions—share types of questions to use. Engage the Receiver in solving the problem. Focus on what the other people are saying to help you stay in touch.

Is That What I Heard You Say?

Sometimes, tone of voice can change the meaning of the Message. So if you say the same sentence to someone and just emphasize a different word with a different tone or inflection, you can shift the Message.

If you do not believe me, try it for yourself. Read the following sentence aloud, each time emphasizing the bold word as you read it. Can you hear the different meanings? Jot down what meaning you receive from each sentence.

I really enjoyed dinner last night!

Meaning: ⎯⎯⎯⎯⎯⎯⎯⎯⎯⎯⎯⎯⎯⎯⎯⎯⎯⎯⎯⎯⎯⎯⎯⎯⎯⎯

I **really** enjoyed dinner last night!

Meaning: ⎯⎯⎯⎯⎯⎯⎯⎯⎯⎯⎯⎯⎯⎯⎯⎯⎯⎯⎯⎯⎯⎯⎯⎯⎯⎯

I really **enjoyed** dinner last night!

Meaning: ⎯⎯⎯⎯⎯⎯⎯⎯⎯⎯⎯⎯⎯⎯⎯⎯⎯⎯⎯⎯⎯⎯⎯⎯⎯⎯

I really enjoyed **dinner** last night!

Meaning: ⎯⎯⎯⎯⎯⎯⎯⎯⎯⎯⎯⎯⎯⎯⎯⎯⎯⎯⎯⎯⎯⎯⎯⎯⎯⎯

I really enjoyed dinner **last** night!

Meaning: ⎯⎯⎯⎯⎯⎯⎯⎯⎯⎯⎯⎯⎯⎯⎯⎯⎯⎯⎯⎯⎯⎯⎯⎯⎯⎯

I really enjoyed dinner last **night**!

Meaning: ⎯⎯⎯⎯⎯⎯⎯⎯⎯⎯⎯⎯⎯⎯⎯⎯⎯⎯⎯⎯⎯⎯⎯⎯⎯⎯

Resist the urge to critique too quickly. Listen for what is not being said and try to eliminate assumptions. To listen for what is not being said, you have to be an active listener and fully engage in the listening process.

Difference Between Listening and Hearing

Anyone can hear, but listening is difficult. Listening is making a conscious effort to hear or attend closely. Listening is processing. It requires patience, practice, attention, and a conscious effort.

Hearing is passive, while listening is active. We are always hearing, but what we need to do is be a better listener.

To help you understand what I mean by hearing and listening, let's assume you are commuting to work with someone.

You are driving in the car with a co-worker and you have the radio on in the background. You and the Receiver are talking about the big project coming up for a client. During this conversation, you are passively hearing the radio in the background and actively listening to the person talking to you.

Then suddenly your favorite song comes on the radio. Unbeknown to your passenger, you start actively listening to your favorite song on the radio and passively hearing your friend. To your friend, you look like you are paying attention to her. But you have just made the shift from listening to her to hearing her.

Passive Hearing

I meet people every day who think they are actively listening, but they are really just passively hearing. Here are a few examples of passive hearing.

Has this happened to you? You walk in an office and you yell across the room, "Good morning!"

The person on the other side of the office shouts back, "Fine, thank you." Listening or Hearing? The person you were talking to heard what you said, but did not really listen.

I went to this fast food restaurant one time and said to the server, "I'd like a cup of coffee and a piece of pie." The server quickly responded with, "Would you like any dessert today?" Wait, I had just ordered dessert. The server must have just attended the "push the dessert" seminar where they were trained to ask every customer if they would like dessert. Since they were so focused on selling dessert, they did not listen to my order.

Finally, I read this in Reader's Digest about four or five years ago, and it stuck with me. There is an epitaph on a tombstone in Vermont that reads, "See, I told you I was sick." Listening or hearing?

Do You Hear What I Hear? Why It's So Hard to Be an Active Listener

Do you hear what I hear? Our brain can process information faster than people can speak. This gap is what makes us either good or poor listeners. Listening is a learned skill that involves utilizing the gap between how fast we think and process information and how fast others speak.

If you want to be a better listener, let me tell you the secret. The secret is each of us has a Genetic Attention Prohibiter (GAP). This is the gap between how fast someone can talk and how fast you can think.

We think at a different speed than we speak.

Take a guess at how fast we think and how fast we speak:

We think at _____ words/minute.

We speak at _____ words/minute.

> ## World's Fastest Talker
>
> Fran Capo, comedienne, adventurer, author, and motivational speaker, is best known as the World's Fastest Talking Female. She holds the record of 603.32 words per minute. Now that is fast!

The average person talks at a rate of about 150 words per minute, while we can listen at a rate of up to 450 words per minute. On average we can think three times faster than we can speak, thus causing a GAP. What you do with the gap is going to determine whether you are a good or a poor listener.

> ## IMPACT Insight: Pets Are Better Listeners?
>
> 1/3 of pet-owning married women said their pets are better listeners than their husbands, according to an Associated Press poll in April 2010.
>
> 18% of pet-owning married men said their pets are better listeners than their wives are.

What would your significant other say about your listening skills? How about your customers?

Poor Listener

Think about someone that you know who is a poor listener.

What are some of the things that poor listeners are doing with the gap between how fast they can think and how fast the other person can speak?

_____

_____

_____

Here are some examples of what poor listeners do with the gap. Mark the ones you see yourself doing. Poor Listeners:

- [ ] Don't focus on what the person is saying, but think about what they are going to say as soon as you shut up.

- [ ] Go off on tangents—they hear one thing and it makes them think about something else. The next thing you know, minutes could go by and you do not know what they are saying because you got lost in your own world.

- [ ] Interrupt to talk about themselves.

- [ ] Assume they know what you are going to say.

- [ ] Complete your sentences. You cannot even say two words and they jump in to complete your sentence.

- [ ] Daydream.

- [ ] Never listen, they just talk. (I have a T-shirt for them. Remember the TV commercial, "Help, I've fallen and I can't get up!"? Here is the T-shirt, "Help, I'm talking and I can't shut up!")

- [ ] Argue with what you are saying.

- [ ] Ask too many questions and even personal questions that have nothing to do with the topic.

- [ ] Get defensive.

- [ ] Change the subject (back to them).

- [ ] Compete for talk time.

Good Listeners

If, as an extrovert, I can learn to become a better listener, anyone can. The first step is shifting your perspective from one of knowing to one of learning. Instead of listening to respond, you listen to understand and learn first.

If you want to be a better listener, here is what you can do. Take this gap between how fast we think and how fast others talk, and do something with it.

Now take a minute and think about someone that you know who is a great listener. When you are with them, you know you are being heard.

What are some of the things that the good listener is doing with the gap?

List some examples here:

_____

_____

_____

All of us have this gap. You are born with it. It is inevitable that you are going to have a challenge to be a good listener.

What can you do with the gap? Utilize your gap to concentrate on what is being said.

How can you do that? Here are nine things good listeners do:

1. Focus on the main points.

2. Do an internal summary.

3. Ask questions.

4. Keep the conversation moving.

5. Watch their non-verbal communications.

6. Do not interrupt

7. Be curious.

6. Do not judge.

9. Do not take things personally.

Your Questions Drive the Conversation

A woman in one of my workshops came up to me during a break and told me about her son. "My son is a freshman in college and I noticed that, when I call him to see how he is doing he doesn't share much. His answers are very short. For example, when I ask him, 'How was your week?' his reply is, 'fine.' Or if I ask him, 'Are your classes going well?' his answer is 'yes.' 'Did you have any tests this week?' His response was 'no.' Do you have any suggestions?"

Well, I could tell right away what the problem was. It was not about her son's answers; it was about her questions. She was asking closed-ended questions: "How was your week?" and "Did you have any tests this week?"

Sometimes when a conversation is not going well, the first place to look is you. What can you do differently to improve this communication?

I asked the woman to give me an example of an open-ended question she could ask. She said, "How was your week?"

I asked her, "What are you—more introverted or extroverted?"

She responded quickly, "More extroverted."

I said, "I could tell because for you, 'How was your week?' would be a good question. For your son, who is more introverted, 'How was your week?' is a disguised open-ended question. You need to ask a more direct, open-ended, question because he still could answer, 'Fine.'"

So I told her, "Listen, next time your son calls, open the conversation with a direct open question, one that tells and not asks. For example, 'Tell me about your week?' Then pay attention to your follow-up questions. Make sure you avoid as many closed-ended questions as possible."

A month or so went by and I had actually forgotten all about our conversation until I received an email from her. She wrote:

Dear Mr. Donadio,

I wanted to write to thank you for your advice about how to get my son to open up more when I call.

The last few phone calls went great. He is telling me more about school and all his activities. I realize now that all I had to do was be a more active listener, including paying attention to the types of questions I ask him.

In fact, I have even noticed that my conversations at work are going better. It is amazing what a few simple techniques can do.

Thank you for the great workshop.

Best wishes, Mary

Challenging Versus Inviting Questions

Closed Questions (challenging)	Open Questions (inviting)
Are you responsible for this error?	What can you tell me about this issue?
Will this step solve the problem?	How can we make sure this will solve the problem?
Are you going to meet the deadline?	What would help you meet the deadline?
Have you finished the ABC Project?	Where are you on the ABC Project?

Can you see the difference between open (inviting) questions and closed (challenging) questions? What emotional differences do you notice between the two?

Open questions are less threatening and more likely to maintain or deepen the relationship than the closed questions. I am not saying we should never ask closed questions. They are great tools, especially when trying to redirect the conversation with an extrovert. Simply be careful how you ask them so as not to threaten or make the listener feel defensive.

Here are some closed questions. Try rewriting them as open questions.

1. (Closed) Is this the biggest challenge we have?

(Open)

_____

_____

2. (Closed) Can you finish it this week?

(Open)

_____

_____

3. (Closed) Does Mary fit into the team?

(Open)

_____

_____

Listen to Understand, Not Respond

What did you say?

Could you please listen?

Have you heard these questions before? Not being a good listener can cause challenges, missing work assignments, and people getting frustrated with you. When we listen, we want to be focused on listening to understand what is being said.

Sometimes we are so busy listening so that we can respond that we don't hear what the other person said. If you are doing tactical planning in your mind while someone else is communicating with you, you are hearing, but not listening. You are too focused on your "me" agenda.

> *"From listening comes wisdom;*
> *from speaking comes repentance."*
>
> — *Italian proverb*

IMPACT Insight: Me-Focused or Other-Focused?

The most important person in any conversation should be the other person. Pay attention to how often you are me–focused or other–focused in your conversations.

Find ways to focus on the other person more. Keep a journal of what you notice. Here are a few questions you can ask yourself:

- What drives you to the "me" mode?

- How did you catch yourself and how can you catch yourself sooner next time?

- When you catch yourself, what can you do to shift from me-focused to other-focused?

How Can You Be a Better Receiver?

The following techniques will help you actively get involved in the listening process and help you listen to understand. Some of these techniques you may already know. However, the question is, are you using them? Remember, it's not what we know; it's what we do with what we know. If you read one of the techniques below and you say to yourself, "Oh, I know that," then ask yourself a second question, "Am I using it?"

To be an active listener, you must engage your entire self into the process not only by focusing on the words, but also on the Receiver's facial expressions, posture, voice, eyes, and gestures.

The following techniques will help you actively get involved in the process. As you read the list, focus on any ideas you tend not to use on a regular basis and put them into practice:

1. Before the Conversation (Active Mind)

Being a good listener happens before the conversation even starts. Here are a few ways to get ready to be a better Receiver before the conversation:

- Get mentally ready – Clear your mind of any preconceived idea that could taint your understanding of the Speaker's message. Be open-minded. Temporarily let go of your need to be right and any prejudices you may have.

- Come prepared – Develop a list of questions you want to ask. This gets you in the asking or listening mode. Developing questions in advance ensures that you will gather the information you need.

  "People don't care how much you know until you show how much you care."

  — Zig Ziglar

2. During the Conversation

During the conversation, you can be a better listener by engaging physically, mentally, and by being part of the solution.

Physically Engage in the Communication

- Listen with your eyes – Some studies show that up to 80% of the message can be non-verbal. So by not only focusing on the words, you can engage your whole self into the process. Make eye contact with the person and pay attention to non-verbal cues. Notice their emotions, energy, and then explore them further with questions.

- Watch non-verbals – It's not always what you say, but how you say it. Watch the Sender's non-verbal communications. Look for eye contact, change in voice, facial expressions, posture, tone of voice, gestures, and so forth. Does what they are saying match their body language and their voice? Any mismatched signals could give you more insight. Remember, more than half the Message is non-verbal. So when in doubt, check it out.

- Make eye contact – What do we know about communication now that we took the survey? 80% of your message is not what you say, but how you say it. Therefore, if you are not looking at the person and making eye contact, guess what, you might be missing half of the Message. What else can you do to be a better Receiver? Jot down a few notes on an index card and try them this week..

- Mirroring – This is a technique where we might model or mirror what the Sender is doing in terms of not only posture, but even voice or pace. If somebody talks very fast, you might talk a little bit faster. If they talk slower, you might talk a little slower.

Mentally Engage in the Communication (Active Mind)

- Think before responding – Suspend judgment; think about what the Receiver said before responding.

- Take notes – When appropriate, take notes. This is an active way to stay engaged in a conversation. However, take brief keyword notes. Writing too much while listening can hinder your listening skills. Your notes will be a good tool to jog your memory later.

- Pauses are a great skill – Do not be afraid of silence. People process at different speeds and they may be hearing it for the first time while processing the information. If you ask too many questions and do not leave space, they may not be able to digest all the information. As a coach, I am not paid for what I know. I am paid for helping the client process the information and come up with his or her own answers, a skill that leaders should also embrace.

- Pauses may seem uncomfortable, but do not automatically interject your comments. Senders may need a little time to gather their thoughts. Silence shows strength. Give them a chance to hear themselves.

- Internal summary – Concentrate on what is being said and try to summarize the main points in your mind. Listen to understand, not to respond. Focus on what the Sender is saying and inside your brain, say, "So they said this, and then they said that, and then they said this." What you are doing is putting together a jigsaw puzzle in your mind. You are trying to get all the pieces together and when you can't get a piece, what do you do? You ask a question.

- Minimize distractions – Do not try to take phone calls, read e-mails, or complete another task while the Sender is talking to you. Remove any obstacles that may divert your attention and do one thing at a time -

INTENTION

MESSAGE

PERSON

ACTIVATE

CLARIFY

TRANSFORM

listen to the person. Multitasking diminishes our capacity for listening.

- Don't interrupt – Let the Sender finish what they are saying. Moreover, think about it before you respond.

Be a Part of the Solution, Not Part of the Problem

- Encourage the Sender – Make the Sender feel heard. Your body language can be an encouraging or discouraging factor when getting others to talk. So demonstrate your interest by leaning forward slightly, making eye contact, being physically attentive (not doodling, squirming in your chair, or looking at your watch), and giving encouraging, natural, vocal cues (for example: "Mmm," "Interesting," "Really?" "Then what?" "Wow").

- Be Curious – Listen to learn, not to respond. Be an inquisitive Receiver. Ask questions to learn more.

- Restate – For clarification, repeat what the Sender just said using their words. For example, "Let me repeat this to make sure I understand." Check out the words as well as the significance of the words. Then wait for the Sender to confirm or clarify your restatement.

- Paraphrase – This technique is where you restate what the Sender said in your own words to see if you understand the message. "So let me see if I understand, you would like me to..." or "So it sounds like you want...." Then wait for the Sender to confirm or clarify your paraphrase.

- Ask questions – We may think listening is passive. We think, "I'll just sit there and I'll listen for a few minutes." However, listening is not passive; it is active, and asking questions is a part of the listening process. Be an Active Listener. If you don't understand something, wait for a break in the conversation, politely interrupt, and ask a question focused on the topic at hand:

  - Ask questions to clarify what the Sender is saying.

  - Asking questions shows the Sender that you are interested and engages them in the conversation.

  - Ask open-ended questions – Encourage Senders to tell you more examples like: "Tell me more about that?" "What do you mean by that?" Or force them to think through an idea. "What do you think we could do?"

  - Ask closed-ended questions to move along the conversation. With some people, they ramble on and it is hard to find the main point. Therefore, by asking questions, you can figure out the main point they are trying to make.

- Avoid prejudging – Listen in a nonjudgmental mode. Get all the facts before you draw your conclusion. Don't assume you know what the Sender is talking about until you heard the whole message. We sometimes have a tendency to see what we want to see and hear what we want to hear. Try avoiding phrases like "That will never work," "We tried that before," or "Stop, I know exactly what you're going to say."

- Avoid tuning out – Be careful not to tune out because you may disagree with what the Sender is saying. Remember, your job is to listen and understand, not necessarily agree. This is especially true when listening to a complaint or description of a problem.

- Concentrate – Take an active approach, focus, and concentrate. That is a difficult thing to do.

- Timing – If it is not a good time to talk, say so. Reschedule when you will be more focused.

- Don't take things personally – As soon as you start to take things personally you will have a tendency to become defensive. Your defensive mindset will drive the way you listen and respond.

It is important to be aware that if you want to be a better listener, it is not just going to happen. It will take a little bit of effort on your part. These are a few ways you can become a more active listener.

> *"Remember that silence is sometimes the best answer."*
>
> — *The Dalai Lama*

In Business, Listening is Gold

One of the keys to success in business is providing your customers with a quality product or service.

If I asked you, "What does quality mean to your customer?" what would your response be?

I hope that you would not fall into the trap of just generically answering this question. To find out, you have to listen to your customers for the answer.

"Quality" is whatever the customer says it is. If you want to provide quality, you have to listen to what the customer is telling you because only they define quality. The customer may want it fast, they may want the best price, and/or they may want the best product regardless of price. Only the customer can truly define what quality means for them.

If you are making assumptions about how the customer defines quality, you probably will not provide the best quality for the customer. So in order to define quality, you must first listen to your customers, which means you will want to ask them questions to uncover their needs and wants.

> *"If speaking is silver, then listening is gold."*
>
> — *Turkish proverb*

As the proverb says, listening is gold, and that especially applies when it comes to business. In order to better serve our customers, deliver quality service, and make more money, we need to be better listeners.

Better Listener

If you want to be a better Receiver, then you may want to use some of the ideas I just shared. Ask questions, watch for non-verbal actions, do an internal summary, focus on the main point, or repeat back to the person to make sure you heard correctly.

All of us can benefit from being a better listener. It is not just going to happen because you read these ideas. It is only going to happen when you begin to practice some of these skills.

Write down the name of the Person that you want to be a better Receiver to, a deadline on when you are going to practice, and some techniques you want to use with this person.

Name: _____

Date: _____

Technique(s) to practice: _____

_____

_____

_____

Now when you get back to work, apply these skills with this person and start improving your listening!

Activate Your Group Communication

In addition to face-to-face conversations, many of us also spend time each day communicating with groups.

Activating your communication is just as important, if not more important when you give a speech, make a presentation, conduct a meeting, or present a teleconference.

Engage Your Audience

You are sitting in the audience and looking at your watch wondering, how much longer will I have to sit here? The speaker has only been speaking for about ten minutes and you are ready to leave. Have you been in this situation recently?

Audiences want to be engaged. The old days of a talking head standing in the front of the room pontificating behind the lectern are long gone. The professor-style lecture does not work anymore, not even in the classroom. People want to be engaged mentally, physically, and emotionally.

> *"I am always ready to learn, although I do not always like being taught."*
>
> — *Winston Churchill*

Add "Commercials" to Your Presentation

We live in the instant generation: instant coffee, instant oatmeal, and fast food drive-thru. At my house, we have instant entertainment at our fingertips – we can choose from almost 1000 cable television channels. If I do not like what's on one channel I can switch to another, another, and another.

We have a similar impatience while sitting in audiences today. If a speaker doesn't immediately engage us, we will change the channel, tune them out, and start tuning into other channels (tasks, worries, concerns, wishes, fears) that have nothing to do with the presentation.

Our job as Speakers is to harness any impatience our audience may have and have each person tune into the channels we direct them to.

Television shows have commercials every 8-12 minutes. So if your audience is used to shifting attention because they have been programmed by television, then let's use this strength.

I suggest that we Activate our presentations, and every 8 minutes or so, we should try to shift what we are doing, in order to keep the audience actively engaged.

Various Ways to Activate Your Presentation

Activate your presentation and keep your audience engaged physically, mentally, and emotionally.

Here are some techniques to help you add pizzazz to your next presentation, speech, or public announcement:

- Use Quotes – Find unique quotes from celebrities, audience members, the CEO, a family member, and even add a few of your own into the mix. Each quote is something that the audience can hold onto and then think about as you speak. You can also project the quote in front of the room on a slide or print it on your handout.

- Stories or Real-Life Examples – People relate to people, so share your heart and be authentic when you tell stories. Try to use your own stories whenever possible and do not simply memorize a story. Retell the story as if you are experiencing it for the first time.

- Use statistics and dates –Don't just use numbers; bring them to life. (Each year, over 600,000 people are affected by _____ . You could fill the Ohio State University Stadium six times with all the people who are affected.)

- Ask challenging questions – Get the audience involved mentally by asking questions. This increases their retention. You can ask questions before you discuss something to get people to think and explore the topic and/or you can also ask questions after to help people understand and apply the topic or information.

- Give a quiz – Give either an oral or a written quiz. It could be a short true/false quiz or a multiple choice questions quiz.

- Use a handout – Make an interactive handout. Add spaces/lines for people to take notes. Occasionally leave out key words in a sentence or statement for people to fill in.

- Small group exercises – Get people to share in groups. They can be as small as two or as large as 10. The exercises can run anywhere from a 30-second introduction to a 20-minute case study discussion. Be creative—you can have people answer a question, discuss an issue, solve a problem, or share their experience in a small group setting.

- Magic – Using magic is a good way to entertain people and make a point. You can buy inexpensive, easy-to-do magic tricks and make them tie into your topic.

- Use a visual or prop – Use slides, flip charts, video, and/or posters to reinforce the main points. Props are also a great way to add pizzazz to your presentation. Props can be real-life items that pertain to your topic or larger-than-life items to make a point or get people to laugh.

- Ask for a show of hands – Ask the group informational questions in order to challenge them to see what other people believe, think, know, or don't know.

- Leave time for questions – This allows the audience to learn more and helps you to see if you are on target.

- Use yourself – Shift the pace and engage the audience using yourself:

    - Use your voice – to make a point, from a whisper to a yell and everything in between. Your voice will help keep the audience interested.

    - Use your body – Facial expressions (smile more often), hand gestures, movements, and eye contact are all ways to illustrate a point. Do not stay in one place the whole time; occasionally speak from the left side and right side of the room and even go into the audience.

    - Use your emotions – Show your excitement, frustration, sadness, confusion, etc. This helps the audience see you as a real person.

    - Get them laughing – There are many ways to be entertaining: stories, jokes, cartoons, bumper stickers, and more. As Jeffrey Gitomer wrote, "At the end of laughter is the height of listening."

Warm up the audience

I have learned from experience that if you want to engage the audience, you should "warm them up" first. Here are a few techniques you can use to get them primed to participate:

- Hand each person an index card as they walk into the room and ask them to write down one or two questions they would like to have answered today during our meeting or program.

- Instead of just asking audience members to participate individually aloud at the beginning of your presentation, warm them up first. One way to do this is to ask them a question on their handout and have them write down their answers to your question first. This allows the audience time to think about their answers before participating. This increases their comfort level thus making it safer for them to speak up.

- Another way to warm them up is to have the audience discuss the question with a partner or in a small group first. Then ask them to share their answers aloud, again giving them time to think and build their participation comfort level.

- Ask specific questions to the group instead of generic questions. Do not ask, "Do you have any questions?" Instead ask, "What do you think will get in the way of you using these new skills?"

- Set up ground rules at the beginning of the workshop and explain how participation will work. For example, "Today's program is very interactive. I see myself more as a facilitator and want to encourage participation, so we can learn from each other. One of my goals for us today is that each of you speak up a least three times so we can better learn from each other."

- Reward participants with a prize. Even a small one can be effective. When people speak up or ask a question, give them a piece of candy, a trinket, or even cash as a reward for their participation.

"I hear and I forget;
I see and I remember;
I do and I understand."

— Confucius

Activate Your Meetings by Facilitating Dialogue

Meetings are another arena where you may actively want to get the attendees involved.

Here are seven suggestions:

1. Be supportive, manage differences, and facilitate conflict. Ask questions like:
   - "What are your feelings on this?"
   - "Why do you think we should do it that way?"
   - "Is there a consensus on this issue?"
   - "Aren't we a little off the subject?"
2. Ask both open and closed questions. Example:
   - (Open) "What are some ways we could do that?"
   - (Closed) "Do you think this (issue, item) will offend anyone?"
3. Clarify or paraphrase to clear up any misunderstandings.
   - "It sounds as if the problem is a lack of communication between two staff members. Is that correct?"
4. Reinforce and acknowledge positive participation.
   - "I think that is a great idea; can you expand on that a little more?"
5. Distinguish fiction from fact. Ask for concrete examples.
   - "So you never get any support?"
   - "How much is too much?"
6. Be supportive of new ideas.
   - "That sounds like something we should look into."
7. Get input from people closest to the issue.

- "Is there anything we have forgotten?"

Slides Tips

Many times we may use slides to engage the audience. Remember, use visuals to reinforce the message, not to be the message.

Too many presenters have a slide full of words that they are using as their notes. If the slide is too cluttered it distracts from the message.

18 Tips for Improving Your Visuals

There are a variety of programs out there you can use to create slides, like PowerPoint, Keynote, Prezi, and Slideshare, just to name a few. The following guidelines will help you make sure your slides are there to add to the message and not distract the audience.

Content

- Maximum one slide per minute (even less if it is not a very technical presentation).
- Maximum six lines of text per slide. No more than six to eight words per line.
- Slide should correlate with content of speech.
- Use headings for your slides. The heading font should be between 36 and 44 point.
- Use font size of 24 point or larger. Any smaller font will not be able to be read easily by the audience.
- Have your Main Body Font be between 28 and 32 point.
- Make your Sub-Point Font between 24 and 28 point.
- Use proper capitalization. Text with upper and lower case is much easier to read than all capital letters.
- Use numbers or letters, not always bullets when listing items. This makes it easier to refer back to an item on the slide.

Visuals

- Use of Colors – Stick to the same color for all titles and a second color for the text. You could use a third color on words you want to emphasize and/or for bullets.
- Slide backgrounds – Select colors that have high contrast so text and graphics can be easily seen. If using a dark background such as navy blue or dark green, then choose a light text color such as white or yellow. This

makes the text float on top of the background. If you are using a light background, use black, dark blue, dark green, or a deep red (like maroon) for easy readability.

- Use charts, graphs, or graphics to help clarify points and keep your audience's attention. Pie charts are great to demonstrate percentage relationships. Bar Charts help clarify links between data and Flow Charts/Diagrams help people see the correlation between components or explain systems.

- Keep diagrams simple. If complex, provide it to the audience in a handout and/or break the diagram into two or more slides. When using a handout, be sure to put your contact information on each page.

- Keep animation and sound effects to a minimum. This could be more distracting than helpful.

- Build or reveal your bullet points from the same direction on each slide. Do not use too many different transitions.

Delivery

- Talk to the audience, not the screen. Do not read every slide verbatim.

- Go to a blank or black screen between slides when telling a story or giving an example not found on the slide. To do this in PowerPoint, you can either hit the "B" key for black or the "W" key for white when in the "slide show" mode (hit it once and it goes to blank screen hit it again and the slide comes back on) or build in blank template slides. This will help keep the audience focused on you and your speech, not your slide.

- Have a Backup Plan - Print out a copy of your slides and bring them with you in case the projector malfunctions or the bulb burns out. Also, have a spare bulb just in case.

SUMMARY - Activate

The first step in the Action Phase (ACT) is the Activate principle. Now that you planned and crafted your message in the Planning Phase (IMP), it is time to Activate the message to keep both you, the Sender, and the Receiver engaging and participating in the communication process in order to fulfill your Intention.

Activate yourself so you can listen attentively and engage the Receiver so they will help you achieve the Intention you set for this communication.

Whenever possible, you want to Activate the Receiver physically, mentally, and emotionally.

In the next principle, Clarify, we will talk more about how you make sure that the message you communicated is the same one they received.

IMPACT Insight (Activate)

Here are a few insights from this chapter. Which ones do you want to focus on this week? An active communicator asks great questions, is a good listener, uses stories or examples to keep the receiver engaged, and makes the Receiver part of the solution.

Activate your message by making sure you and the receiver are physically, mentally, and emotionally engaged in the communication.

Mindset drives behavior, so activate your right mindset: adult mode.

Communicate in 3-D, the three dimensions of your message: your words, voice, and non-verbal communication which brings the message to life.

Listen actively with your eyes (for non-verbal), ears (for words), and heart (for emotions).

Active listening is "real" listening. Active listening requires patience, practice, presence, and persistence.

Good Listeners utilize the gap between how fast someone can talk and how fast you can think to stay focused.

Your Questions Drive the Conversation – Use a good mix of open and closed ended questions.

Activate your presentation and keep your audience engaged physically, mentally, and emotionally every six to eight minutes.

INTENTION

MESSAGE

PERSON

ACTIVATE

CLARIFY

TRANSFORM

IMPACT Reflection (Activate)

Here are some questions to help you get ready to Activate your message:

"What mindset will best help me accomplish my Intention?"

"Which of the three forms of communication (spoken, non-verbal, or written) will I use to communicate with the Receiver?"

"Do I have a communication preference? What is my Receiver's communication preference?"

"How will I stay actively engaged in the communication?"

"What is my biggest challenge when it comes to being a better listener?"

"What types of questions could I use to activate the Receiver and help us both achieve the Intention?"

"Do I have a preference when it comes to questions I ask? Open or Closed-ended questions?"

"How will I engage the Receiver mentally, physically, or emotionally?"

IMPACT Application (Activate)

Below are lists of various situations where you may want to apply the Activate principle in your daily routine. Pick one or two that are applicable and list a person, situation, and time when you want to apply this principle.

Presentation (examples: Staff meeting, committee update, board report, training seminar, speech, etc.)

Person: _____

Situation: _____

Date to Apply Principle: _____

Interpersonal Communication (examples: Conversation, phone call, luncheon, etc.)

Person: _____

Situation: _____

Date to Apply Principle: _____

Marketing/Sales Communication (examples: Sales call, luncheon, presentation, etc.)

Person: _____

Situation: _____

Date to Apply Principle: _____

Public Communication (examples: Social media, radio/television interviews, video conferences, etc.)

Person: _____

Situation: _____

Date to Apply Principle: _____

INTENTION

MESSAGE

PERSON

ACTIVATE

CLARIFY

TRANSFORM

Clarify (klar'ə fī') – verb

to make or become clear and free from impurities

to make sure the message sent is the same message received

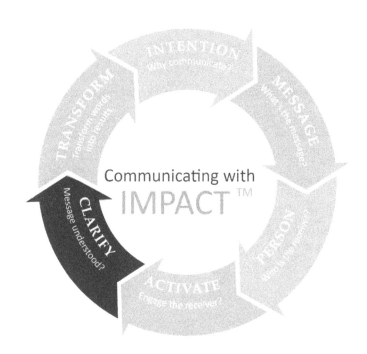

PRINCIPLE 5
Clarify

- Selective Perception
- Six Ways to Clarify your Communication
- Challenges with Written Messages
- Handling Questions
- Four Types of Questions
- Loaded Questions
- False Premise
- Ladder of Intervention
- Non-Questions
- Hypothetical Questions
- IMPACT Insight
- IMPACT Reflection
- IMPACT Application

PRINCIPLE 5
Clarify

"Make sure the message you sent is the same message they received."

C is for Clarify

Is your message understood? Now that you Activated the Message and both Sender and Receiver participated in the communication process, there still is no guarantee that you both received the same message.

So, how do you make sure the message you sent is the same message the listener received? You clarify.

Do You Ever Make Assumptions that You Know What the Other Person Wants?

I only missed one speaking engagement in the past two and a half decades of my professional career and it was for the birth of my daughter. Here's how it happened.

It is not unusual to book a speaking/training engagement a year or more in advance. That was the case with one of my new university clients. They booked me for an engagement with them for next November. A few months after I scheduled the university program, we found out that my wife was expecting our second child. And yes, the due date was right around the time of the program.

I knew better than to risk it, so I called the client and informed them of the situation and told them I would have one of my colleagues on standby just in case we needed him. I called and asked my friend Tom to hold the date for me, and he agreed. Of course I thought, "But there is a slim chance I would need him."

Months went by and now it was the day before my university program. I was gathering my notes and getting ready to go upstairs to pack when my wife informed me that her water had just broken.

"What?" I asked in disbelief.

Well, with little notice, I called my friend, Tom, who came right over. I gave him a brief overview of the program, handed him my notes, and off he went. We made it to the hospital in time and later the next day, our beautiful little girl, Marissa, was born.

After the event, I called Tom and asked him how the program went. He said, "It went okay, considering the short notice."

I knew I needed to call the client and discuss the situation. What should I do about this? I considered carefully what I would say. My initial plan had been to apologize and tell them I was not going to charge them for the program and would pay Tom out of my pocket.

Then it dawned on me. "Why should I make the decision for them?" My intention is to serve the customer and the best way for me to do that is to ask them what they want me to do, and let them decide. After all, quality is whatever the customer says it is!

I called and talked with the client for a few minutes about the program. Then I dropped the all-important question on her. "So, what would you like me to do?"

Her response amazed me. "Nothing," she said. "As a parent, I totally understand. I would have felt terrible if you made the trip here and then missed the birth of your daughter. Don't worry about it."

I was so glad that I had empowered my client to make the decision. I had been prepared to take a loss on this event, and now it turned out that I did not need to do that.

> *"A man hears what he wants to hear and disregards the rest."*
> — *Paul Simon*

Lesson Learned

I learned two lessons from this whole experience that have served me well in my business and personal life.

First, you never know what someone else is thinking, so do not assume the message you sent is the same message they received. That is why this principle is so important.

When in doubt, check it out!

Second, fixing a mistake can actually build a deeper relationship. Yes, mistakes can ruin a customer relationship. However, if handled correctly, resolving the error can actually deepen the relationship. In this case, not only did the client hire me to come back the next year and teach the same program. For the next eight years after that, they remained a loyal client of mine.

IMPACT – Selective Perception Quiz

Below are four questions that are often used in Selective Perception research. Read each question and answer immediately before moving on to the next question.

(See answers on following page.)

1. You are participating in a race. You overtake the second person. What position are you in?

Now answer the second question, but don't take as long as you took for the first question....

2. If you overtake the last person, then you are...?

Do the following question in your head only. Do not use paper and pencil or a calculator. Try it.

3. Take 1000 and add 40 to it.

Now add another 1000. Now add 30.

Add another 1000. Now add 20.

Now add another 1000.

Now add 10. What is the total?

Final question.

4. Mary's father has five daughters: Nana, Nene, Nini, and Nono. What is the name of the fifth daughter?

Answers can be found later in the chapter.

Source: *I Fail to Miss Your Point* by Jim O'Bryon

*"I know you think you understand what you thought you heard
me say, but I'm not sure you realize that what you heard is not
what I meant."*

- Robert McCoskey

Selective Perception

Did you know that up to 80 % of communication is screened by the Receiver?

Many times the meaning of the message comes from the Receiver, not from the Sender. The Receiver subconsciously screens the information based on his/her personal history, interests, background, experience, attitudes, etc. This is known as selective perception.

Even if you communicated effectively, the message sent is not always the one received. That is why we need to check for comprehension. How do you rectify this? You Clarify!

IMPACT Insight: *If yuo can raed this...*

Then yuo uesdnatnrd waht phaonmneal pweor the hmuan mind hsa. Rscheearch shwos it deosn't mttaer in waht oredr the ltteers in a wrod are, the olny iprmoatnt tihng is taht the frist and lsat ltteer be in the rghit pclae. The huamn mnid deos not raed ervey lteter by istlef, but the wrod as a wlohe. Amzanig!

Never Assume Anything

Whether you communicate with people in person or in writing, the Receiver will screen a good percentage of your message.

As the Sender, don't assume just because you communicated the message that they received it as intended.

As the Receiver, even if you think you know what they said, you still may want to Clarify.

You can Clarify in a variety of ways. The key is to take responsibility for the clarity of the message.

INTENTION

MESSAGE

PERSON

ACTIVATE

CLARIFY

TRANSFORM

Selective Perception Answers

#1 Answer:

If you answered first, then you are wrong. If you overtake the second person, you are in second place.

#2 Answer:

If you answered second to last, then you are wrong again. How can you overtake the last person?

#3 Answer:

Did you get 5000? The correct answer is actually 4100. Feel free to check it with a calculator!

#4 Answer:

Her name is Mary. If you got that one wrong, go back and read the question again!

Clarify your Communication

Here are the six ways to Clarify your communication:

1. When in Doubt, Check it Out

Often, people can be incongruent with what they are saying. Their words may not match their non-verbal communication (tone or body language). So, when in doubt, check it out. Be curious and ask some questions. Try to understand the person before you try to communicate. Above all, listen without judgment.

Here are a few sample ways to "check it out":

- "Tell me more about that"
- "If you were in my chair, what would you ask?"
- "I am curious. You are saying you are okay, yet you are still crying?"

2. Unloading Technique - Part I - The Technique

A co-worker or client is coming to talk with you about a decision you made. As you look at them, you can see they have something pressing they want to tell you and they cannot wait to blurt it out. It almost looks like they are about to explode.

In this situation, you have two choices. One, you could start talking to them about the situation and why you made that decision. Alternatively, you could let them talk.

If you say, "Just a minute, let me tell you why I did that," the other person is not going to listen to you. Their head is already full of stuff that they need to unload. So let them! That is what I call the "Unloading Technique." You allow them to unload the stuff on their mind so that there is room for your stuff when you start talking.

Here is how it could work. You say, "Tell me what you're thinking," and then you listen.

That is the entire technique. Simple, right? Let them unload so they can let the stuff out of their cluttered mind, and whatever you say will have a much better chance of sinking in.

The other side benefit of this technique is it also builds rapport because you are listening to them, a rare event these days.

Word of Caution – this may take longer than you might like with an extrovert. Set a mental time limit on how long you will let the extrovert talk and then find a way to transition from listening to talking.

Unloading Technique - Part II - Transition from Listening to Talking

After you use the Unloading Technique, and have let all emotions run their course, you will probably be able to build a bridge to rational discussion. At this point, move from listening to talking.

First, thank the sender/speaker, and then transition from listener to talker. For example, say, "Thank you. That was very helpful, and let me add…."

The following are a few more tips for beginning a conversation after the Unloading Technique and/or anytime you want to move from being a listener to a talker.

- Use the person's name.

- State or restate your purpose. "My priority is to help you solve this problem."

- Indicate you have listened. "I am glad you brought this to my attention. Let me make sure I understand exactly what happened."

- Ask questions for clarification, to check for accuracy, or to hear the information again. This also reinforces that you really mean what you said.

- Use transition phrases to build rapport. When moving from listening to talking, try the following phrases:

- "Well, I understand and…."
- "Well, I appreciate that and…."
- "Well, I know what you mean and…."
- "Well, I agree with that and…."
- "Well I know you're upset and…."

3. Restating Technique

For clarification purposes, just repeat what the person just said using their own words. For example, "Let me repeat this to make sure I understand…."

Check out the words as well as the significance of the words. Then wait for the other person to confirm, "Yes that is what I meant," or clarify your restatement, "No what I really meant was…."

Another way to do this is just to repeat back the whole sentence. For example, if a person says to you, "I never get any support," you could repeat back, "So, you never get any support?" and then pause. The key here is to be patient and wait for a response.

4. Expounding Technique

The Expounding Technique is a tool to get the other person to tell you more so that you can make sure you understand what they are saying.

The key here is to ask open questions (as discussed in the Activate section).

Sign at Dry Cleaners:

Drop your pants here and receive prompt attention.

Is this what they really meant?

Always Ask

Over the years, I have learned that it doesn't hurt to ask. I once had a boss who told me, "When you ask, you will get one of three answers. Yes, No, or Maybe. Two out of three is not bad." Ever since then, I have always asked.

This is also true when negotiating. The following are a few of my favorite questions when trying to negotiate:

- "Could you do any better?"

- "Do you have any specials today?"

- "Is that your best offer?"

- "What else could you do for me?"

Negation Example

I recently made a hotel registration at a national chain for a convention I was going to attend a few months later.

Instead of doing it on their website, I decided to call their toll-free number. When I reached the customer service representative, I said, "I want to book a room for the XYZ Convention. Could you tell me what the group rate is?"

The representative told me, "It is $149.00 per night."

I responded, "Okay, I would like to book a room for three nights." I realized at that point that I had forgotten to ask whether there might be a better rate.

Normally, when I am attending a convention, I will take the group rate, because it is the best deal, and the group organizing the event is counting on members to occupy these rooms. However, this time I asked my favorite negation question, "Is that your best rate?"

The representative responded, "Let me check."

What happened next is what surprised me most. She came back on the line and told me that the regular hotel rate for that particular weekend was $129.00, which was $20 cheaper than the group rate for the XYZ Convention.

"What?" I responded, with a shocked tone in my voice (another good negotiation technique).

"Yes that is unusual," the representative said. "Let me look a little deeper into this. Hold on, please."

The representative came back a few minutes later with some startling news. "Mr. Donadio, I see that there are two group rates. One is $149.00 and the other is $74.50. There are only a few of the $74.50 rooms left. Let me update your reservation to this new group rate."

Sometimes it pays to ask.

> *"Before I came here, I was confused about this subject. Having listened to your lecture, I am still confused - but on a higher level."*
>
> — *Enrico Fermi*

5. Rephrasing Technique

Another technique to employ after you have listened to the other person is a tool I call the "Rephrasing Technique." After your conversation partner is finished speaking, you attempt, in your own words, to repeat back to them what they said. That way you can check for understanding.

This technique is often used in counseling or therapy, and is therefore often referred to as the "counseling technique" or the "psychology technique." In couples counseling, a psychologist would have one person say to the other, "What I hear you saying is...."

You do not have to use that exact question, but it would reassure the Sender that you were listening and receiving their message.

Another few ways to ask this question might be:

- "It sounds like...."
- "From what I hear you saying, it appears...."
- "Let me see if I understand. You would like me to...."
- "If I understand you correctly, you want me to...."

Once you rephrase the answer, then the next step is to wait for the Receiver to confirm or clarify your paraphrase.

IMPACT Insight: Quiz Time

The meaning of your message does not necessarily come from you; it can come from the Receiver. Here is a quick quiz I use in my workshops to help illustrate this point.

Take out a piece of paper and draw the seven lines as shown below (or write in the book...It is okay!)

———   ———   ———   ———   ———   ———   ———

Now write the word DONADIO in the spaces above.

(Then turn the page to see the solution.)

6. Perception Check Technique

A perception check is simply when a Sender asks a question to make sure the Receiver understands what they said.

One way to check for perception is to use the Rephrasing Technique and then follow up the rephrased statement with a question that clears up any possible stray assumptions.

The technique looks something like this: "If I understand you correctly, you want me to...(Place rephrased statement here). Is that correct?"

I saw a poster that illustrated this technique. On the poster there was a picture of an old woman sipping a glass of wine while sitting on the patio with her husband. A caption above her head read, "I love you so much, I don't know how I could ever live without you." A caption above her husband's head read, "Honey, is that you or the wine talking?" Her caption then replied to his, "It's me...talking to the wine."

Perception Check is also a good technique to use when you might see incongruence between what the Sender is saying aloud, and with their non-verbal language. For example, if you notice someone looks nervous, you might ask, "You look nervous. Is everything okay?"

> "The problem with communication... is the illusion that it has been accomplished."
>
> — George Bernard Shaw

Solutions to the Quiz

There are at least four different ways I have seen my name written in the spaces. They look something like the following:

1. <u>D</u>   <u>O</u>   N   <u>A</u>   <u>D</u>   <u>I</u>   <u>O</u>

2. __D_O_N_A_D_I__O

3. D__O__N_A_D_I__O_

4. <u>DONADIO</u> <u>DONADIO</u> <u>DONADIO</u> <u>DONADIO</u> <u>DONADIO</u> <u>DONADIO</u>

What just happened? I gave you one message and we had at least four different perceptions of that message.

Again, who puts the meaning to the message? You, the Receiver, do. So be sure to Clarify to make sure that you both get the same message!

Remember when composing any written communication, there is no immediate feedback. This increases the chance for "selective perceptive perception" to occur. My philosophy on written communication is that, the more complicated the message, the less you want to rely totally on written communication alone.

If you find yourself needing to communicate regarding either a complex or emotionally charged issue, I suggest you use more than written communication. Whenever possible, use at least two modes of communication and move to the telephone or in person communication as soon as possible.

Challenges with Written Message

The message you send may not always be the same message received. This is especially true in written communication, since it is linear and no one is there to give feedback.

Here are a few amusing examples of written communication. You can see how they might be misinterpreted.

Insurance Claim Form: "I pulled away from the side of the road, glanced at my mother-in-law, and headed over the embankment." (He must really hate his mother-in-law!)

Church Bulletin: "Low Self-Esteem support group meets tonight. Please use back door." (That is not going to help their self-esteem much!)

Classified Ad: "Tired of cleaning yourself? Let me do it." (Yikes! I hope they were talking about house cleaning!)

Classified Ad: "Dog for sale: eats anything and is fond of children." (Does this dog eat children? That won't help it get adopted!)

Handling Questions

One of the best ways to check for understanding is to allow people to ask questions. Whether it is in a one-on-one situation, during a presentation, at the end of a presentation, an informal Q&A session, or even a media interview, allowing people to ask questions and knowing how to handle questions is a critical part of this principle.

Different Types of Questions

Here are four examples of the more difficult types of questions you might encounter and some tips on how to handle them:

1. A Loaded Question

We have all heard of loaded questions. The most commonly asked loaded question is, "Are you still beating your spouse?"

If you answer yes, then you are still beating your spouse. If you answer no, then you used to beat your spouse. As you can see, either way you are in trouble. A loaded question is a question that makes an assumption that may not be true.

I was doing some media training for the physicians and staff at a large university hospital. Because the university hospital is a teaching hospital, they would occasionally get a loaded question like this: "Is your hospital still perceived as giving less than quality care because it is a teaching hospital?"

2. False Premise

A false premise question is a question that is based on faulty information.

I was doing some training for the Department of Education of a nearby state some years ago, and one of the false premise questions was, "Why does the State Department of Education feel the need to dictate standards for the local level?"

At the time, this premise was incorrect.

When you get a false premise question, your natural tendency is to want to correct the misinformation. This could get you into trouble, especially if you fall into the trap of believing that the person asking the question is upset or angry with you.

One of the pitfalls to watch out for when handling a false premise question is taking the question personally. Thus, the first step to handling a False Premise question is to make sure that you do not take it personally and become defensive.

Sometimes a loaded question and a false premise question can look very similar, so you use this technique to handle both. Here is a technique to handle a false premise question.

Use the Ladder of Intervention Technique to Handle a False Premise

Many times I will be asked to be the keynote speaker at an organization's annual meeting. Whenever I speak at an event, I like to arrive early and listen to the speaker before me. Once, when speaking at a state teachers' conference, the speaker before me was talking about a technique called the "ladder of intervention." The speaker, who was also a teacher, said that teachers often use this approach when they were trying to deal with a disruptive student. This is also a good technique to use with false premise or loaded questions.

Let's go back to the false premise question, "Why does the State Department of Education feel the need to dictate standards for the local level?"

You can answer this question using the Ladder of Intervention technique. There are two ends of the ladder, Nice and Mean. When you take the question personally, you tend to want to start at the Mean end of the ladder. The speaker/teacher suggested starting at the Nice end of the ladder and then progress your way down the ladder to a Strict/Mean approach.

The following are some examples of how to move down the ladder when handling a false premise question:

Nice (Start here and work your way down)

- "I am so glad you asked that question—that's a common myth we hear quite often. The truth is _____"

- "Perhaps I can clarify that for you."

- "Well, that is not exactly true."

- "Where did you get that information? That is not correct at all. The real truth is _____"

Strict/Mean

As you can see, the way you phrase your answer changes the way it is received. If you start at the strict/mean end of the ladder, you might turn what was an innocent question from an audience member into a controversial issue for the questioner and the audience.

As the song says, "A spoonful of sugar helps the medicine go down."

3. Non-Questions

Sometimes when you are taking questions, you may have an individual who makes a comment instead of asking a question.

If you are not listening carefully, you may mistakenly think their comment is a question and begin to answer it. This may take you off the subject or lead you down a path that you may not want to follow.

For example, after a presentation someone raises their hand and says they have a question.

"I think that there is already too much time spent on evaluating employees."

Notice they really have not asked you a question. How do you respond? When someone presents a non-question or a statement, you have four choices:

1. Pause, smile, and basically ignore the comment and wait for the question.

2. Ask for clarification if this is an issue you want to discuss. "I am not sure I understand your question. Can you repeat it please?"

3. Agree with the comment if it reinforces your point. "Yes, I totally agree with you!"

4. Use the comment as an opportunity to bring up an important point that relates to your topic. This is called the bridge technique. Where you bridge from their comment to a point you want to bring up by using bridging words like and, also, because, in addition, and so on.

For example: "Yes, I agree and that is why starting next quarter we will be implementing a new program to help managers improve their leadership communication skills."

As you can see, a non-question can also be an opportunity in disguise. Their comment can actually open the door for you to discuss a topic you want to talk about yet was not asked.

4. Hypothetical Questions

A hypothetical question is when someone tries to draw you into a future scenario by asking a question about a future result or outcome.

Be careful not to be drawn in by the hypothetical question because it is usually difficult to predict the future.

Here are a few ways to handle hypothetical questions:

1. Don't answer the question:

   Question - "What if the economy continues to decline, what would you do then?"

   Answer - "Not being an economist, I'd rather not speculate about that."

2. Focus on what you know to be true:

   Question - "If sales continue to decrease within the next year, would you propose a staff cut?"

   Answer – "I'm confident that this is just a temporary slump."

3. Turn the question into a question that you can answer:

   Question - "What if you find that the new product is not well received?"

   Answer - "If you are asking me, 'Am I concerned about the sales of our new product?' Then the answer is no. We have done extensive market research that shows there is a definite need."

I hope now that when you hear a question that starts with the words "What if," you have a few more ways to handle that question.

SUMMARY - Clarify

We see what we want to see and we hear what we want to hear.

It does not matter how well you talk or how well you listen. If the Sender and the Receiver don't both get the same message, then you have not communicated effectively.

This key is an important part of the process. Without clarity, it will be difficult to transform your words into actions and your actions into results.

Clarification is also a way to test for commitment or agreement and start the transformation process.

"How well we communicate is determined not by how well we say things, but by how well we are understood."

—*Andrew S. Grove*

IMPACT Insight (Clarify)

Here are a few insights from this chapter. Which ones do you want to focus on this week? Keep in mind your Intention for this communication as you wrap up your conversation and check for understanding.

It doesn't matter how well you talk or how well you listen. If the Sender and the Receiver both don't get the same message, then you haven't communicated effectively.

The meaning of the message comes from the Receiver.

You never know what someone else is thinking. When in doubt, check it out!

Fixing a mistake can actually build a deeper relationship.

Allowing someone to unload or share their insights helps you clarify what is really going on and makes room in their brain for your information when you start talking.

Clarify by repeating what the person just said, using their own words. For example, "Let me repeat this to make sure I understand...."

Ask Questions. "When you ask, you will get one of three answers: Yes, No, or Maybe. Two out of three not bad."

Remember, written communication is linear and no one is there to give feedback, so it is more prone to misinterpretation.

Be careful not to be drawn in by the hypothetical question, because it is usually pretty difficult to predict the future.

INTENTION

MESSAGE

PERSON

ACTIVATE

CLARIFY

TRANSFORM

IMPACT Reflection (Clarify)

Here are some questions to help you apply the Clarify principle and make sure the message you sent is the same message they received:

"Do I realize that the meaning of the message comes from the Receiver and not me, the Sender?"

"What is my default mode? Do I check for understanding to make sure the message I sent is the same one they received? Or do I assume that, since I am a good communicator, they got it?"

"Which Clarification tools did I find most valuable? How many of them did I know but was not using?"

"Do I find myself using linear communication (emails, texting, IM) as my default mode of communication? Even when I am dealing with a complicated or difficult message?"

"If I am an extrovert, do I remember to leave time for questions? Better yet, do I let the other person talk?"

"If I am an introvert, do I remember to ask questions when I do not understand something?"

"Am I keeping in mind my Intention for this communication as I wrap up my conversation and check for understanding?"

IMPACT Application (Clarify)

Below are lists of various situations where you may want to apply the Clarify principle in your daily routine. Pick one or two that are applicable to you and list a person, situation, and time when you want to apply this principle.

Presentation (examples: Staff meeting, committee update, board report, training seminar, speech, etc.)

Person: _____

Situation: _____

Date to Apply Principle: _____

Interpersonal Communication (examples: Conversation, phone call, luncheon, etc.)

Person: _____

Situation: _____

Date to Apply Principle: _____

Marketing/Sales Communication (examples: Sales call, luncheon, presentation, etc.)

Person: _____

Situation: _____

Date to Apply Principle: _____

Public Communication (examples: Social media, radio/television interviews, video conferences, etc.)

Person: _____

Situation: _____

Date to Apply Principle: _____

INTENTION

MESSAGE

PERSON

ACTIVATE

CLARIFY

TRANSFORM

Transform (tran(t)s-fórm) – verb

to change in form, appearance, composition, or structure

to convert one form of energy to another form

to convert words into action and action into results

PRINCIPLE 6
Transform

- I+B+A = Transform
- Transform from the Outside In? Or the Inside Out?
- Transform From the Outside In?
- Three Important External Tools to Transform Your Message to Results
- When is the Communication Over?
- Single Cycle IMPACT Process
- Multiple Cycle IMPACT Process
- Transform from the Inside Out?
- Four Important Internal Tools to Transform Your Message to Results
- End with the Intention
- IMPACT Insight
- IMPACT Reflection
- IMPACT Application

INTENTION

MESSAGE

PERSON

ACTIVATE

CLARITY

TRANSFORM

PRINCIPLE 6
Transform

"Communicating is not just about information; it's about how you use the information to transform ideas into action to achieve your Intention."

T – Transform

How do you Transform your words into action to achieve your Intention?

In order to transform your words into action, you also have to transform yourself. In other words, you need to change the way you think about your intention, your actions, and your relationship with the other person.

Even if you do use all the other keys in the IMPACT process, there is still no guarantee you will achieve the Intention you set. The final key, Transform, is what moves the process forward. It completes the cycle and turns your Intention into reality.

Have you ever found yourself communicating about the same issue over and over again and still not understanding or seeing a change in behavior?

In today's multitasking, electronic communication world, effective communication is more important than ever. Everything we do or achieve involves communicating. We think we are saving time by responding quickly in the fast-paced world we live in. However, are you really saving time?

Some people assume that they can just sit down and pump out a quick email, pick up the phone and quickly return a call, or even get up in front of a group and convey their idea without any planning time, and still communicate effectively.

The few extra minutes you invest in walking through the IMPACT process with your communication will pay off in the long run in terms of the results you achieve and the time you save.

How to Transform?

When I conduct communication training with individuals and businesses, I go through hours of instructions about understanding each step in the IMPACT process, the tools you can use, and the studies to support this. But at the end of my program, I like to simplify it to one thing: taking action. This isn't really complicated, what I call taking action is simply about how we turn our communication into results. You cannot achieve your Intention unless you take some form of action. I have a very simple model to show what it takes to Transform words into action. I call it the Transform key.

I+B+A = Transform

Three elements make up the Tranform key. The synergy of all three, your Intention, plus your Beliefs, plus your Action, working together is what makes it possible to transform your words into action to achieve your Intention. We talked about the Intention in our first chapter, and in this chapter, I will be exploring the other two components of the Tranform model: Beliefs and Action.

Transforming your IMPACT

Let me briefly review the IMPACT process again before we dive into the last step.

I – Intention.

"Think before you speak." Before you say a word, pick up the phone, send that regretted email, write that note, or send that tweet, know where you are going. Take a few moments to think about why you are having this communication and what you want to have happen as a result of this Intention.

M – Message

Craft your message based on your focused Intention and choose the right method to communicate that message. If your intention is to discover information, then you would want to ask more questions and do less talking. If you want to build a deeper relationship, then you might want to meet in person or have a phone call instead of sending an email.

P - Person

Adjust your communication message to the Person (Receiver). For example—Never hug an engineer. Think twice before asking an extrovert, "How are things going?" Avoid making an introvert get up and make an impromptu speech. Remember to practice the Platinum Rule®, "Treat people the way they want to be treated."

If communicating with an analytical, be sure to come prepared with facts and data. If he or she is an extrovert, be sure to use stories and examples to keep his or her interest. The better you know the person and their communication style, the better you will know how to make this interaction help you achieve your intended results.

A- Activate

Find ways to activate your message in order to engage yourself and the other person in the communication physically, mentally, and emotionally. People today have shorter attention spans, so find ways to engage the other person. Go from a blabbermouth to an active listener, from control freak to letting others participate, from being the center of attention to letting another person be in the limelight.

C- Clarify

Did you both receive the same message? Check to see if they understood you and if you understood them. You don't want to be the person who sees someone nod and assumes they agree, or who doesn't summarize the conversation because you think you were clear about what you wanted, even if you weren't.

T- Transform

That brings us to the last step in the IMPACT process: T- Transform. What transformation can you make so that you get what you intend, and successfully achieve your goals? What do you say and do to make sure the intention happens?

Transform - Build on the Momentum

Even though Transform is the sixth and last principle of the Communicating with IMPACT process, transformation occurs throughout, not only at the end. Activity is initiated in this principle, but emotional and intellectual transformation must begin much earlier in the process.

Let me take the IMPACT process and walk you through a real scenario to show you the process in action from both sides of the conversation, his and mine. I will use the example of one of my coaching clients, a CEO of a Fortune 500 company.

I – My Intention for this coaching project is to help the CEO take his presentation skills to the next level. We started this process by identifying three specific outcomes for the coaching. His overall Intention is to be better at delivering his message.

M – For him, the Message is drafted by his communication staff. For me, the goal is to help him take their message and make it his own.

P – For me, I need to know him as a Person better so I could coach him more effectively. For him, he needs to understand who he is (his strengths and areas for improvement), and to whom he is communicating so he can better adjust the message to his listeners. For his communication staff, they need to know more about the CEO and his preferences so they could work better together.

A – For me, I need to be a better active listener and ask better questions. Many CEOs like coaching better when they can be in the driver's seat. For him, since we are working on delivery, he needs to learn how to Activate himself, his message, and his audience more effectively.

C – I want to Clarify in order to make sure he understands me and I understand him. He wants to make sure his audience understands him.

T – We laid down all the main ingredients to Transform our interactions into making his Intention a reality. I want to transform him into a more powerful presenter by using the tools I shared. He wants to transform his audiences by sharing his message.

Transform from the Outside In? Or the Inside Out?

If you want to Transform your words into actions and your actions into achieving your Intention, you need to ask yourself two key questions:

1. What has to happen externally to Transform this communication into results?

2. What has to happen internally to Transform this communication into results?

Transform from the Outside – Doing

Let's start by exploring the external transformation. This is the area most people are familiar with and may already be doing. Three key ingredients of the outer transformation are:

1. Date/Time

2. Action

3. Feedback

These components are the starting point of transforming your words into actions and your actions into achieving your Intention.

Here are three important external tools to Transform your message into results:

1. Mutually set deadlines for the goals to be completed.

2. Break down goals into action steps.

3. Build in a feedback loop.

1. Mutually set deadlines for goals to be completed

Setting deadlines is an important way to make sure the transformation takes place. Once you clarify what is to happen next, you have to help make it happen. Without action, the results may never occur at all. Without deadlines, getting the results tends to take longer.

Yes, you are probably thinking, "Come on Donadio, this is Communication 101!" Yes it is. However, many leaders still make assumptions about deadlines. They assume you should have known "I wanted this done today," or that "as soon as possible" is a clear deadline. Or because they are the leader, they should set the deadline. Have you had a communication this week where you could have been clearer about the deadline? I will bet the answer is yes.

Here is where leaders can take this one step further: you can, as a leader, engage others in developing a time frame, and co-create deadlines together.

For example, you could tell the Receiver that you need to have the assignment done by Friday at 4:00 p.m. However, what if the Receiver is juggling a few other projects? By forcing them to complete the assignment by Friday, you might get a result on time, but sacrifice the quality of the result in the process.

What if instead you mutually set the deadline by involving the Receiver in the process? You can do this by simply asking, "When could you get this assignment done?" Let's say they come back with, "I could get this done by Monday," and you initially wanted it by Friday. One extra day might be worth the wait to get a better, quality result.

2. Break down goals into action steps

Not every communication will have or need action steps. However, if it does, one simple way to start thinking about breaking a goal into action steps is to use the "outcome thinking" approach I discussed in the Intention chapter.

- Break the goal or task down into manageable parts with deadlines to each.

- Be sure to link the parts back to the organization's strategies and goals.

- Use measurement tools such as scorecards, dashboards, or the action planning tools at the end of this chapter to measure and show progress.

- Do not confuse activities with results. As you wrap up your communication, this step helps ensure that you transform words into specific actions that lead to the attainment of your intention.

Create a written action plan.

When you are dealing with a more complex issue, a large project, or a relational style person, I suggest you consider jotting down a few notes so you can assist in the creation of a written plan.

Some messages you send, like written communication or email, will already have your ideas captured. However, if you had a phone call or a conversation, and you did not take any notes during the communication, I suggest you make record of your ideas as soon as you finish the communication.

In order to create an effective Action Plan, you will want to ask yourself and/or the Receiver a few questions:

INTENTION

MESSAGE

PERSON

ACTIVATE

CLARITY

TRANSFORM

- **What action** needs to/will be taken?

- **Who** will be responsible for each action? You? The Receiver?

- **When** will these actions need to be completed?

- **Why** will these actions not take place? What roadblocks or barriers will get in the way of the completion?

- **How** can I assist in the achievement of the Intention? What do they need from me?

- **Any other questions pertinent to the completion of the action(s).**

I am a big believer in keeping it simple. You can write a ten-page document or use some comprehensive project management software. Moreover, for some projects, these are necessary. When it comes to communicating with IMPACT, a simple list of action steps will suffice. You or the Receiver can create this list. And just as we discussed, by mutually setting deadlines, you could also help the Receiver create the plan.

Sometimes I just record the answers to these questions on my electronic calendar, and other times I create a special tracking form, noting each step and exactly who will do what by when (see sample Action Plan below). What we are looking for is whatever it takes to transform our words into action.

Sample Written Action Plan

I held various leadership roles prior to starting my business and found taking notes to be an effective way to transform my words into action. One example is when I worked as a university administrator. I had nine direct reports and I used to have weekly one-on-one meetings with each of my staff. In order to help me remember my conversations with each person, I created a simple form to help me track my communication with each of them. I actually created a similar form that I still use with each of my coaching clients to help me remember what we talked about in our coaching sessions and to track what the client agreed to do between now and the next coaching session.

There are some cool electronic tools you could use, but I found that a simple one-sheet worked great.

Here is a sample of what a written action plan could look like:

Action	Who	When	Roadblock/ Barrier	Need from me?
Complete project evaluation	Tom	Aug 6th	Time Management	Help pri- oritize/give feedback

3. Build in a feedback loop

Regular feedback reduces the margin of error; so work to develop a reporting system to catch small problems before they become big problems, just as airline pilots do when flying on long international flights. Pilots constantly have to keep that plane on the flight path. Even though they may set the plane on autopilot, they still need to keep an eye on the coordinates and make small course corrections along the way for wind and possible computer errors.

Hypothetically, if the pilots did not make these course corrections and allowed the plane to stray off course, the plane might end up landing in China, Russia, or even Alaska instead of its final destination, Tokyo. The same is true in our daily communications. Even though we know our Intention (destination), we may not end up there unless we keep making small course corrections by gathering feedback and staying connected.

IMPACT Tip: Explore Solutions to Uncover Barriers

Effective leaders use great questions to empower employees to uncover information. When an employee comes to you with a challenge, instead of giving them an answer (the default mode for many leaders), ask them a question instead.

Here are some of my favorite coaching questions to help people identify, define, and begin to create solutions and avoid potential roadblocks:

- What obstacles might you meet along the way to taking these steps or meeting this goal?

- What will you do to deal with or eliminate these internal and external barriers?

- Who else needs to know what your plans are? How will you keep people informed?

- What support do you need? (People, skills, resources, coaching, assistance, etc.) From whom do you need this support?

- Have we missed anything? Is there anything else you want to talk about now or are we finished?

Feedback loops create ownership and allow for course correction. It is important to build in a feedback loop to make sure that the issue gets resolved not only in a timely fashion (meeting the deadline), but also in an efficient manner. So make yourself available. You can give feedback in person, on the phone, or by email. Getting the Receiver to help create the feedback loop increases their ownership in the process.

IMPACT Insight: Summarize for Success

Every time you have an important communication or one that may be a little complicated, you want to make sure that the message you send is the same message that they receive. There are two ways to summarize. Either you can summarize or you can let the Receiver summarize. Either way, in a transforming summary, you should include the following:

- The main points discussed

- What actions will be taken or need to be taken?

- Who will be responsible for each action?

- What is the time frame/deadline for each action?

Summaries might begin like:

- "Just to make sure I was clear, let me review the key issues...."

- "I know I covered quite a bit of material; here is what I want us to focus on as we move forward...."

- "Before we leave, briefly tell me which of the items you (we) are going to be doing as we move forward."

- "So from your perspective, what are the key elements that you (we) need to focus on?"

When is the Communication Over?

Is the communication over when you wrap up the conversation? When you hang up the phone? When you hit send? When you finish taking questions? When you both agree on the direction you are heading?

None of the above! The communication is over when your Intention is fulfilled.

Common Non-Transforming Closings

- Your closing is your final chance to create transformation – to make sure you achieve the original Intention you set. Here are a few examples of ineffective closings: "Thank you," "Do you have any questions?" "Does that make sense?" "I'll send you something," and "I'll stay in touch."

- How do you close to create some movement toward your Intention?

- Don't hover! Leave the person alone to get on with the work, but be available to answer questions.

- Follow up as needed in formal performance review conversations or informal conversations.

Single Cycle IMPACT Process

Communication can happen in a single cycle of the IMPACT process or it can take multiple cycles. It can be as simple as going through the process once and you nail it (see diagram).

For some communications, when you finish a brief interaction, your intention will be fulfilled. An event is one example of this.

INTENTION

MESSAGE

PERSON

ACTIVATE

CLARIFY

TRANSFORM

DONE!

Communicating with IMPACT™

Single Cycle Communication Closings

The goal here is to condense your entire conversation into 30 seconds. Hard to do? Yes. Sometimes you might need 60 or 90 seconds. However, once you craft this, you are on your way to uncovering the core components for your closing. Your closing should leave the listener feeling as good, if not better, than when you met. The brain responds better when it does not feel threatened.

REMEMBER: Without a powerful closing, you may find yourself turning a single cycle process communication into a multiple cycle communication and/or having a similar conversation again and again to get the result you want.

An event has a clearly defined beginning and end and can be accomplished in one communication.

Let's say you have a conversation with a coworker to decide what issues to cover at the next staff meeting. If this was the only Intention for the conversation, once your decision was achieved, this Intention is accomplished and there is no need to build in a feedback loop because the Intention was already accomplished.

Multiple Cycle IMPACT Process

Many times we may think of communicating as a single cycle, but it might take a few cycles, a few interactions with the receiver, before we completely achieve our intention.

The first time through the cycle, you may find that you have not achieved the Intention you set or that the Intention you set is not really the Intention at all. If this happens, you run through the process again, this time paying attention to which IMPACT key needs to be fine-tuned or what you might have missed.

At first, the progress might go well, and you might think the communication is over. Remember, the communication is not over until you have achieved the Intention you set.

Communicating with IMPACT™

(Cycle diagram with: INTENTION, MESSAGE, PERSON, ACTIVATE, CLARIFY, TRANSFORM)

Multiple Cycle Communication Closings

Here are three alternative closings to help you gather more information and/or move the conversation forward:

1. If you are not sure what the next step is, put them in charge of the movement. You can do this by asking a simple open-ended question: "So what's the next step?"

2. If you feel you have enough information, you can take charge of the movement by making a suggestion or recommendation of the next steps, followed by a few questions to Activate them into the conversation: "Based on what you shared, here is what I recommend we do...." Follow this with a question: "What do you think?" "How does that sound to you?" "When would you like to get started?"

3. Or you can delay action and schedule another conversation to answer their questions by asking, "When would be a good time to get back together so I can present you with a few options?"

INTENTION

MESSAGE

PERSON

ACTIVATE

CLARIFY

TRANSFORM

Transform from the Inside Out – Being versus Doing

We have talked about what you have to do in order to transform your message into results. And this is all important, but the truth is, you could spend all day working the principles in this book: the I, the M, the P, all the way to T, and still have only moderate success. However, if you want mega-success, you have to understand that it is not only what you are DOING that makes an impact, but also how you are BEING. Are you following me here?

There is a difference between Doing and Being. Doing is the act of making something happen. Being is the energy we bring to every act of doing. It is the background, foundational influence on our actions that occurs whether we are paying attention to it or not. The problem is we spend so much time focusing on what we need to be doing that we fail to pay attention to how we are being. Until now.

Everything you Do has a Being attached to it. Let me repeat that, Everything you Do has a Being attached to it. For example, imagine you go into a meeting and you are in a Being state of boredom and disgust about being there. How do you think your Doing is going to play out in that meeting? Compare that same scenario with you going into that meeting with a Being state of positivity and enthusiasm. How might that affect your Doing?

The same goes for when you are having a conversation with anyone. How you are Being in that conversation will absolutely impact the way you are communicating (Doing). And it will show.

When you follow the IMPACT model to communicate effectively on the outside (the Doing) and combine it with how you are on the inside (the Being), transformation happens. In other words, to have an impact on the outside, you have to work on transforming yourself (and others) on the inside. At this point in the journey, it's up to you. Is just working on the DOING enough for you? Or are you ready to take it a step further and work on your BEING? I figure, heck, you have gotten this far, so you must care at some level. Why stop now?

I'm going to walk you through some simple steps to Transform your Being so that your Doing can have mega-impact.

I break this part of the inner transformation process into four parts:

1-Build Awareness

2-Change Beliefs

3-Shift from Why to What & How

4-Trust the Process

I remember taking a couple of psychology classes in college and learning about human behavior and how we create change. Over years of working with clients and numerous hours of coach training, I modified what I learned in college to craft a Change Process Model (CPM) to work with my coaching clients in helping them change to make a greater impact in their workplace. There are several steps in the model, but the ones I want to focus on are our inner Awareness and our Beliefs, and how they can support us in communicating with impact.

Build Awareness

Sometimes the first step to change is awareness. If you are not aware of something, then how will you know whether you want to change it?

In 1987, I had a client who offered to videotape one of my seminars for me. I agreed, and a week later, I received the videotape. I placed it into my VCR and began to watch myself speak.

At the time, I had a mustache, and about every three minutes during my presentation I would reach up with my right hand and touch my mustache just under my nose. As I watched it on video, it looked like I was picking my nose. I felt embarrassed. What was more astonishing was that I never knew I was doing that!

Now that I was aware that I touched my moustache often, I had a choice to make. Continue this behavior or change it? Since this behavior produced a negative result (looking stupid), I decided to change this behavior in hopes to change the result. However, how would I know to make this change if I had never taken the time to reflect and become aware?

Self-reflection is always available. However, how often do we practice this? At the end of a conversation, do you stop to ask yourself, "How did I do? What was accomplished? What could have been better?"

When we take time to ask and answer these questions of ourselves, we are actively looking for ways to be better. This can be tough for some folks, because looking at what needs to be changed can feel like looking for flaws. A better way to approach this is to look for areas that you could stand to improve. For now, just remember that self-reflection is your friend when it comes to making positive changes and communicating with impact. Looking at yourself in a constructively critical light can be a gift to yourself and others.

Sometimes the reflection can be done for you, like when someone offers you some feedback or input on your performance. Other times you can ask for the input to reflect on. Take my client, Bob, who found that he was missing the mark with his team, so he asked the Human Resource Manager for some feedback. Bob was surprised to discover that his staff found him to be "too abrupt" and "cold and callous" in his communication. This was surprising because he always took great pride in his ability to be concise and swift in his delivery (something that was typical back East where he grew up). Now in the Midwest, he realized he needed to adapt to the needs of the people if he was to maintain integrity in his job.

Be open to accepting feedback. It does not matter where feedback comes from, whether the feedback comes from asking yourself questions, someone volunteering information, or you seeking out feedback. The point is you always want to reflect on feedback to build more awareness.

Questions are a key component to transforming. Are you asking yourself the right questions to improve your communication? What do you need to be more aware of for IMPACT to occur?

Once we are clear on the results we want and the actions that will get us there, then we focus on identifying (becoming aware of) what behaviors we need to change in order to get those specific results.

Change Beliefs

One of the biggest drivers behind our Being state is the belief we have about ourselves, about others, about an event, or even the belief we think others might have about us. Yes, the belief we possess drives our behavior. So it stands to argue that Communication with IMPACT is about transforming the words you use (including the ones you say to yourself, your beliefs) into actions (what you do, your behavior) so that you get different results.

Belief About Yourself

The belief you have about yourself will drive your actions. I had one executive coaching client who told me that she was not funny, and that using humor in her presentations made her look unprofessional. As we dug a little deeper, we uncovered that, growing up she had an older brother who was a "smart aleck." She told me how she witnessed first-hand what happened when her brother joked around all the time. He usually embarrassed her and sometimes himself. For this reason she used very little humor. So I asked her to watch how other leaders used humor and see if she thought it made them look unprofessional. Well, she came back to me and reported that she discovered humor, when used effectively, really enhances the relationship the leader had with their employees. We started to explore how she could use more humor. However, I made a little belief shift for her. I told her that what would be even more effective at building relationships would not just be using humor or trying to be funny, but being more entertaining, which encompasses more than telling jokes. Entertaining people means engaging others in the communication by making them feel good, connecting with them through stories and real examples, and actively engaging the Receiver in a way that creates a more memorable experience.

Belief About the Other Person

The more work you can do on changing your beliefs before you head into a conversation, the more impact you will have.

How would your belief about someone impact the way you communicate with him or her? For example, how different would your communication be if you went into an interview believing that the candidate was highly qualified versus poorly qualified? You might think that you can mask any belief you have and that the other person will not hear it in your words. And you are right. They might not. However, they will hear it in your energy. Communication comes in all forms, and a high percentage comes from our non-verbal signs.

This is the same for every day communications. Many times we have preconceived notions or beliefs about the other person and are not even aware of them. What belief shift do you want to make about the other person that will best help them achieve their Intention?

Belief About the Situation

Imagine you are heading to a sales call with a prospective client, and before you leave, your co-worker tells you that that the client's company has no money to spend. He assures you that you will not get the sale and that the sales call will be a big waste of time. How will this impact the way you approach the sales call, perform in the sales meeting, and close the sales call?

Your belief about this situation will definitely affect how you approach the sales call. What type of situation do you face every day? What faulty beliefs might you have about this situation and how might it affect the way you communicate?

Other comments can shift our belief about a situation. We may choose to accept their beliefs as reality. As you are communicating with someone, keep in mind that the belief he or she may have about the situation will have an impact on what they do or not do. What belief does the Receiver have about the action that needs to take place to make your Intention for this communication a reality? Is this a belief that will help them transform this intention into results? If not, how can you help them see the situation differently?

I have been teaching at Notre Dame University in the summer for the past seven years. My first summer there, I went to work out at the Knute Rockne Memorial Gymnasium, a recreational facility for students, faculty, and staff which opened in 1937. They built "The Rock" in memory of Knute Rockne, Notre Dame Football coach from 1918 to 1931 and, by percentage, the winningest coach in college football.

They have a new facility on campus, but I wanted to work out at the "The Rock" because of a story I read about Knute Rockne in the book, *The Magic of Believing*, by Claude M. Bristol. As the story goes, one Saturday afternoon, the Notre Dame Football team was trailing badly at half time. The team nervously waited in the locker for Coach Rockne's arrival. Rockne delayed his arrival to the Notre Dame locker room meeting. The discouraged players wondered where their coach was. Minutes ticked and the half time was almost finished. At the last minute, Rockne slowly opened the door and popped his head into the team room and, with a startled look in his face he said, "Oh, I'm sorry, I thought this was the quarters of NOTRE DAME Football Team." And with that, Rockne closed the door and left. Startled and stung by his brief remarks, the Fighting Irish went out and won the game.

The famous coach understood that the situation the team was facing was influencing the way they were thinking. This belief would influence their second half performance, so Coach Rockne knew he had to remind them of who they really were in order to get them to perform up to their potential in the second half. How can you inspire others to make the changes you know they need to make to achieve the results they need to get?

Shift from Why to What & How

As we move toward transforming our initial Intention into reality, we need to start asking different types of questions both of ourselves and of others.

Up to this point, asking "why" questions were very helpful. Why questions help us focus on defining the situation. Now as we move into the last step, we want to Transform "Why" questions into "What" questions.

"Why" questions uncover the story we tell ourselves about what we think or believe happened and allow us to go deeper into understanding.

"What & How" questions, move us towards focusing on the solution and taking action.

Why is this happening? Why don't we have more clients? Why are we not getting the projects done on time?

Here are a few examples of how to transform "why" questions into "what" questions:

- Instead of asking, "Why is this happening?" ask, "What can we do to stop this from happening?" Do you see the shift from understanding to action?

- Instead of asking, "Why don't I have more clients?" ask, "What can I do to get more clients?" or "How can we get more clients?"

- Instead of asking, "Why are we not getting projects done on time?" ask, "What can we start doing to get projects done on time?" "How can I start getting projects done on time?"

As you can see, one formula is to shift from asking, "Why…" to "What/how can I (or we) do…."

The "what" and "how" questions help us focus more on action and we need some form of action to transform our communication and interactions into results.

Trust the Process

One of the biggest shifts you can make to facilitate the journey towards greater impact is to trust the process, even when it gets tough or feels uncomfortable. Even if you don't get immediate results, you must trust.

This is going to require that you do some things differently. And guess what? It is not always going to be easy. However, it is possible and your chance of success is much greater if you can trust that what you do will actually work.

Imagine doing anything, while inside you are saying, "Why am I even bothering? This isn't going to work anyway." You are energetically calling off any possible progress. Hope is lost. Dreams shattered. Success thwarted.

I have seen the IMPACT process in action, and it works. When you trust, you allow space for error, and you don't let it stop your quest for success. You acknowledge that even though it may be difficult, you know that it will be worthwhile.

One of my clients became frustrated with the progress he was making on his presentation skills. He had some reservation about speaking and never thought he would be any good on stage. Therefore, when we started working together, I had to ask him to trust that he will succeed at this, especially during those times he felt like giving up. And I asked him to trust that if he worked hard enough and long enough, he would be confident on the speaking platform sooner rather than later.

In hindsight, I can honestly say that the work we did together to help him trust the process was equally as important and effective as the work we did on his speaking skills.

We build trust in ourselves and with others throughout the IMPACT Process. By the time we get to the Transform step we have laid a foundation of trust:

- Intention - our initial Intention drives the relationship and builds trust

- Message - the way we present and structure the information, our words and non-verbal cues help build trust in others

- Person - the way we blend DISC personality styles and the rapport we build increases the relationship, which in turn starts building trust

- Activate - the stories, actions, activities, experiences, emotions, and internal thoughts we use to engage the receiver garnishes trust

- Clarify - the questions we use, answers we give, and insights we gain, open the door for trust

- Transform – all of the above lead to helping us transform this interaction/ communication into results

The more trust we have in our common relationship, the more likely the Receiver will take the action necessary to make the Intention we set for our communication a reality. And if this happens, you are sure to be communicating with IMPACT!

End at the Beginning?

The key to truly making an IMPACT is to start with an idea of what impact you want to make. The Intention sets the stage for the transformation to occur.

Now the final impact may be different than planned because in many cases we are dealing with a process, not an event. Yet starting without an intention, we leave the outcome open to chance.

This final key, Transform, is one that runs through the entire process and culminates with the attainment of the intention, no matter how long it takes.

Does that mean you cannot change the intention? Of course not. As you go through the process, you may discover that your original intention was not realistic, or on target, one sided, or win-lose. You might find that, with more insight and understanding, you were off base. Then, by all means, go back and adjust your original intention and run through the IMPACT process again. This is a collaborative process.

When you change yourself, you change your communication. When you change your communication, you change the world, both your inner and outer world.

Trust the IMPACT Process, Trust Yourself, and Trust Others

This sounds counter intuitive, since we do not always have to have a plan. Once you have used the process, it becomes second nature to you. You might just decide to have a conversation with someone and it is amazing to see what transforms.

The process evolves and shows up, and you do not necessarily have to plan it. I meet a lot of people as I travel the globe speaking and training. I never know who I might meet, what questions they might have, or what insights they might share. Trust the process and you will be amazed at what can happen.

After one of my keynote speeches at a convention in Leavenworth, a beautiful resort town nestled in the mountains in the state of Washington, an attendee came up to me and asked, "Are you around later today to talk?"

"Why yes," I replied. "In fact, I was going to grab the box lunch that the convention was providing and go sit by the river. Would you like to join me?" He said yes and we both grabbed our box lunches and headed outside.

As we walked over to the river, you could feel the crisp fall breeze. We found a picnic table and sat down across from each other. I happen to be facing the mountains with a beautiful view of the fall trees changing colors. Eric (not his real name) started to tell me how my keynote jogged his memory about the impact his father had on him when he was growing up. "My Dad never thought I was good enough. He rarely shared any positive feedback with me and seemed to always be critical of everything I would do."

"Do you believe that?" I asked.

"No, not today," he replied.

I paused a moment and then asked, "Are you sure?" Eric looked off into the distance staring at the convention center behind me.

"Well I guess there is a part of me that still does believe that."

This was really interesting, so I wanted to understand more. "Why?" I asked again.

"I am not sure," he quickly answered.

"Could it be that you have been looking more to the past than to the present?" I asked.

"What do you mean?" he answered in a rather frustrated tone.

"Have you received positive feedback from others in the past few years about you or your performance?"

"Sure, why?"

That is when I realized that he needed to shift his perspective about this situation. "Would you mind switching places with me on the picnic table?"

"Why?" he asked.

"Well, I just realized that the view from my side of the bench might help you explore this a little further." So we switched. Now I sat facing the street with the Convention Center in the background and Eric was facing the river and the beautiful mountainside with those fall colored trees.

"What do you notice?" I asked.

"Wow, this is a beautiful view!" he replied with a big smile on his face.

"Which view have you been seeing about yourself? The view of buildings, cars, and cement, or the view of the river with the beautiful mountainside? What view do you think your dad grew up seeing?"

"The street view," he answered.

"Do you think he ever saw the other view?"

"No, not really. In fact, he grew up in a house with a father who drank too much and was not a very kind man."

"Really," I said.

"Yes, and now that I think of it, his view was probably even worse than mine." He paused for a moment and I just sat there. I surveyed the mountainside and I could see he was absorbing this beautiful view. Then suddenly he let out a deep sigh. "I never thought about how my dad's view influenced the way he treated me. I am sure, growing up, he never felt he was good enough. How could he know there was such a view if he never saw it?"

> "Dialogue is a process of genuine interaction through which
> human beings listen to each other deeply enough to be changed
> by what they learn."
>
> - Harold Saunders, founder of the Sustained Dialogue Institute

I could sense that this was an important revelation for Eric. He took in a deep breath and just sat there. It was one of those rare moments when you know something profound has happened. Eric reached up and wiped his eye as he turned and looked at me, "Wow... that was amazing."

"What?" I asked.

"What just happened? I never thought how tough my dad had it and how much better my youth was than his. What an impact this small shift has had on how I view this situation."

What an impact this small shift had. It started an IMPACT cycle inside of him to begin to transform how he thinks and ultimately how he will act.

End with the Intention

End where you started. Come full circle back to the initial Intention for having this communication in the first place.

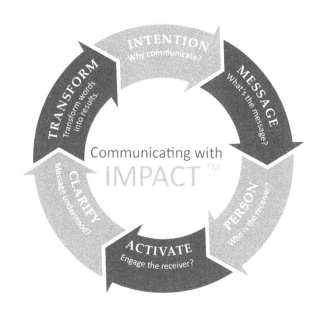

SUMMARY – Transform

Transform = I+B+A

One day my daughter brought home from elementary school a piece of paper, a mini poster of sorts that read:

> *"Watch your thoughts,*
>
> *for they become words.*
>
> *Watch your words,*
>
> *for they become actions.*
>
> *Watch your actions,*
>
> *for they become habits.*
>
> *Watch your habits,*
>
> *for they become character.*
>
> *Watch your character,*
>
> *for it becomes your destiny."*

After doing a bit of research, it appears that Frank Outlaw, Late President of the successful U.S. supermarket chain called BI-LO said this. This leader gets to the essence of the Transform principle.

Not only are we transforming results when we are Communicating with IMPACT, we are also transforming organizations one person at a time.

The synergy of all three elements, your Intention (destiny), plus your Beliefs (thoughts), plus your Action (habits), working together is what makes it possible to transform your words into action to achieve your Intention.

TRANSFORM = INTENTION + BELIEF + ACTION

IMPACT Insight (Transform)

Here are a few insights from this chapter. Which ones do you want to focus on this week?

- Intention +Belief +Action = Transform

- To Transform your words into actions and your actions into achieving your Intention, try asking yourself two key questions:

    1. What has to happen externally to Transform this communication into results?

    2. What has to happen internally to Transform this communication into results?

- Three important external tools to Transform your message to results:

    1. Mutually set deadlines for goals

    2. Break down goals into action steps

    3. Build in a feedback loop

- When is the communication over? - The communication is over when your Intention is fulfilled.

- Is this communication a Single Cycle IMPACT Process or a Multiple Cycle IMPACT Process?

- Transform From The Inside Out - Everything you Do has a Being attached to it. So how you are Being (your Beliefs or state of mind) impacts the way you are communicating (Doing).

- Four Internal Tools to Transform Your Communication into Achieving Your Intention:

    1. Build Awareness

    2. Change Beliefs

    3. Shift from Why to What & How

    4. Trust the Process

- "Why" questions allow us to go deeper into understanding. "What & How" questions move us towards the solution and taking action.

- End where you started: with the Intention!

IMPACT Reflection (Transform)

Once you answer these questions, you are ready to Transform your message into reality.

The Transform principle is one that many communicators overlook. Here are a few questions you should be able to answer to make sure you have achieved the Intention you set for this communication:

"Was there any movement (physically, mentally, and/or emotionally) as a result of the communication?"

"Am I closer to achieving the original intention/result of this communication?"

"If not, what has to happen toward the end and/or after the communication to help Transform my words into actions to achieve the Intention I set?"

"What are the next steps I and the receiver have to take to make this intention a reality?"

"When do these steps need to take place?"

"What obstacles might I meet along the way to taking these steps or achieving my Intention?"

"What will I do to deal with or eliminate these internal and external barriers?"

"What follow-up communication needs to occur? By whom? By when?"

"How will I reinforce any positive behaviors (I want repeated) that occurred to make this Intention a reality?"

IMPACT Application (Transform)

Below are lists of various situations where you may want to apply the Transform principle in your daily routine. Pick one or two that are applicable to you and list a person, situation, and time when you want to apply this principle.

Presentation (examples: Staff meeting, committee update, board report, training seminar, speech, etc.)

Person: _____

Situation: _____

Date to Apply Principle: _____

Interpersonal Communication (examples: Conversation, phone call, luncheon, etc.)

Person: _____

Situation: _____

Date to Apply Principle: _____

Marketing/Sales Communication (examples: Sales call, luncheon, presentation, etc.)

Person: _____

Situation: _____

Date to Apply Principle: _____

Public Communication (examples: Social media, radio/television interviews, video conferences, etc.)

Person: _____

Situation: _____

Date to Apply Principle: _____

INTENTION

MESSAGE

PERSON

ACTIVATE

CLARIFY

TRANSFORM

PUTTING IT ALL TOGETHER

As I walked into the prospective client's office, I could feel my heart beating faster and faster. This person was the CEO of a large organization. In fact, if he were to hire me as his coach, his company would be the largest client I had ever worked for.

Luckily, his administrative assistant, Mary, referred me to him. I met her at one of the workshops I taught at the local university. When she called me to let me know that her boss was looking for a coach, I was immediately interested.

I began by asking Mary some questions to help me prepare.

"Tell me more about John, your CEO? What type of challenges is he facing?"

"What is he like as a leader? As a person?"

"What is the main purpose of his organization?"

"Why is he looking for a coach?"

After the phone call, I had a better idea as to what this project might look like and what other questions I might need to ask John to determine whether this was going to be a good match between us.

Now I was getting nervous because this would be the biggest coaching client I would have to date. Who else was I competing against? What experience did they have? Was I really the right person for this project? Could I achieve what the CEO hoped for?

Suddenly I realized I was acting as if I was not going to get the job. Therefore, I decided to stop trying to make the decision for the client; I would leave it up to him. My job was to determine whether I would be able to work with his company, and to show John the value I could offer if he should hire me. I decided that, even if I did not get the job, this would be a good learning opportunity. Either way, I would win!

With a little less pressure on my shoulders, I now began to prepare for the meeting. At first, I did not know where to begin. Then I decided to use my own coaching tools; why not use my IMPACT process to help prepare? The following is how I put the process into action:

Intention

Beyond my Intention not to show my nervousness, the real Intention was to make sure this client would be a good fit. Since I worked hard to build my business on my reputation, the last thing I wanted to do was to take on a project for which I could not deliver results.

"The first step to solve a challenge is to define it."

Message

As we discussed previously, your Intention should drive your message. Since my Intention was to determine if this would be a good fit, it made sense that the majority of my message would be made up of questions.

I started my research by initially asking his assistant, Mary, some questions to get to know more about the CEO, John, and his situation.

Next, I had to determine what I was going to ask John. I also wanted to think about the five key areas that I would share in order to show him that I had the expertise and experience to help him with his challenges.

Person

Once I had a clear idea of my Intention and a good understanding of my Message, it was time to focus on the Receiver. How would I personalize the Message to blend my style and the Receiver's style?

Mary informed me that her CEO, John, was more analytical and a little more introverted than extroverted. She also informed me that John was an attorney and very interested in details.

Since the Intention for this interview was to determine if this was a good fit, I had to be careful as an extrovert not to do too much talking. That is why coming prepared with a series of questions would be helpful for me. Now that I know the receiver is analytical and an attorney, it would be helpful if I had some data/statistics to back up my selling points, like how many coaching clients I have worked with, the various types of clients, the average length of a coaching project, and so on.

Activate

Now that I knew more about the Person and had a clear idea about my Intention and Message, I move my thoughts toward how to Activate this communication.

How do you stay engaged and how do you engage the Receiver in the communication? The key is to actively engage them mentally, physically, and emotionally.

In this case, the Receiver is a little more of an introvert, and therefore I know I have to actively engage the CEO in the communication. This not only engages the Receiver mentally, but also emotionally and physically as he tells his stories.

At the same time, I have to be careful not to be too engaged myself (a challenge for extroverts). A few ways I have found to help me listen better is to:

- Come prepared with a series of questions.

- Remind myself to shut up.

- Do an internal summary throughout the conversation.

- Take notes during the interview to help me stay focused.

> *"Seek first to understand, then to be understood."*
> *— Stephen Covey*

Clarify

As I am having the conversation, how do I make sure the message that I sent is the same message he receives?

As I said in the C Chapter, many times the meaning of the Message comes from the Receiver, not from the Sender. Yes, you send the Message but it may not be received or interpreted the way you want it to be. Clarifying throughout the communication helps make sure you both get the same Message.

This is where taking notes can come in handy. Here are a few things to consider when you are going to take notes. First, be sure to ask for permission and explain why you are taking notes. For example, "Is it okay if I take a few notes to make sure I get the details down?" Second, be sure to make good eye contact while you are taking notes. I actually have practiced writing while not looking at my paper so I could fine-tune this skill.

Also, good clarifying questions help. "So what I hear you saying is ____" or "It sounds like ____."

Transform

Finally, how do you Transform your Message into action to achieve the Intention? What has to happen after the communication to help with the Transformation?

What are the next steps you and the Receiver have to take to make this Intention a reality? When do these steps need to take place? What follow-up communication needs to occur? By when? By whom? What is the next step?

In preparing for this stage, I found myself thinking of all the questions I might want answered. Some of these questions I can ask earlier if possible. Others are specific to trying to move the conversation along to the next level.

The Outcome

So you are probably wondering what happened. The CEO hired me. Yes, I had my first CEO client and learned a valuable lesson about selling to the C-Suite. You don't sell to the C-Suite, you just help them buy.

My preparation and the IMPACT process made this interaction more comfortable and made me stand out among my competition.

After I was hired, I asked my new client why he hired me. His answer was interesting: "You were the only one taking notes."

"Why was that a game changer?" I asked.

"I wanted a coach who would listen and be focused on my needs and the needs of our organization," he responded. "You demonstrated that by your great questions, listening skills, and your attention to detail."

Whether you are in the boardroom, workroom, lunchroom, backroom, conference room, classroom, media room, or family room, Communicating with IMPACT works.

What's Your Why?

The questions we ask drive where we focus.

What is your "why"? What was your Intention for reading this book? You got this far in the book for a reason. Why?

Why is Communicating with IMPACT so important to you? What areas in your life do you want to use the IMPACT process? What do you want to change? Who will benefit?

The IMPACT process can make an impact in every part of your world.

Of course it is possible to transform yourself and others with this process in your professional life. Also consider your personal relationships, personal joy, personal satisfaction, and even your health.

The bottom line is, when you get better, life gets better.

The better we communicate, the deeper the relationships. The deeper the relationships, the better we become. The better we become, the better results we achieve. The better the results, the greater the IMPACT.

> *"Intention without action is useless."*
>
> — *Caroline Myss*

AFTERWORD
From the author

"Nothing changes until you change!"

If you close this book now and do nothing different than when you first picked up this book, there will be little to no difference in your life, career, and the results you get. Work on changing a few things in your communication in order to achieve the results that you need.

Take a few risks. Do not be afraid to make mistakes. Mistakes are the building blocks of learning. Luckily for you, many of my coaching clients and I have made some of the mistakes for you. These mistakes led to much of what I covered in this book. Remember that your mistakes can be turned into learning opportunities.

> *"When we strive to become better than we are, everything around us becomes better, too."*
>
> *- Paulo Coelho*

Kaizen – Continuous Learning

While in Japan, I visited a Nissan automotive factory. Touring the plant, I noticed a big banner on the wall of the factory. It was written in Japanese but I knew it was something important.

So I asked my interpreter, "What does that banner say?" He replied, "That banner says 'kaizen.' Kaizen is the Japanese word for 'continuous improvement' or 'change for the better.' At this plant they have a philosophy of always getting better." That was my first exposure to continuous improvement.

"How do they do that?" I asked.

"By continually learning from their mistakes," he replied.

Even though I wrote this book on communications, and I am still learning, I wish I could say that every communication I engage in goes perfectly. However, I have found that communication is a skill you never completely master. We are continually learning and it is no different when it comes to becoming a better communicator.

W/D2 Process

After my experience at the Nissan plant, I created a continuous learning process I call "W/D2" to help my clients continue to improve.

Therefore, after every important communication, whether it is a presentation to the board, a conversation with an employee, or even a misinterpreted email, I encourage my clients to apply this simple W/D2 process to help them continually improve.

Here is the simple process to turn every mistake into a learning opportunity. You simply ask yourself two questions:

W - "What did I do Well?" (What will I do again?)

D2 - "What will I do Differently to Develop the next time to improve?" (What do I want to Do More Of? Do Less of? Do Differently?)

I have found that most of my coaching clients start their learning process by focusing on what they did wrong. I created the W/D2 process to force them to find the balance. Simply make two columns and on the left side, jot down what you think you did well, and on the right side, what you want to do differently to develop the next time:

W Well?	D2 Do Differently to Develop

As you apply the IMPACT Process, I encourage you to debrief your communication experiences by using the W/D2 Process. It only takes a few minutes to implement and is critical to getting better in communicating with IMPACT.

IMPACT Insight

To gain a better understanding of how well you have communicated with someone, after communicating with him or her, try asking yourself the following three questions:

1. "Is the message that I am sending the same message they are receiving?"

2. "Has there been any change as a result of this communication?"

3. "Am I closer to achieving the intention I set for this interaction?"

If you answered "yes" to all of these, great! If not, then you have a wonderful learning opportunity.

Learning Opportunities

Transformation is usually a process, not an event. Therefore it takes time, energy, fine-tuning, and repetition to transform words into action and actions into results. Debriefing is a key element in the transformation process. You can debrief during the communication and after it, and there will be many learning opportunities along the way.

> "If you do what you've always done, you'll get what you always got."

> — Mark Twain

We have covered six keys to help you communicate with IMPACT. How do you implement this transformation in your life and business?

My favorite quote is this quote by Mark Twain. I hear it from many people, and I say it to myself all the time. I believe that I can make a difference in my own life by choosing what I do and what I do not do. Yes, knowing what not to do is just as important as knowing what to do.

This is just the beginning. Finishing this book is the start of the process to help you communicate with more impact. You will find that every day you have opportunities to take an ordinary communication and turn it into an extraordinary communication by applying the IMPACT process. I wrote this book to be a guide you can use and refer back to when needed. Keep it close by. It contains the tools necessary to transform not just what and how you communicate, but also what results you get from your daily communication.

If you do nothing differently, you are going to be no different. Everything will stay the same, and you will have made little or no impact.

Remember, "Nothing changes until you change!" Apply the IMPACT Process today and impact your world.

Be in touch.

Patrick Donadio

patrick@patrickdonadio.com

ACKNOWLEDGMENTS

Many people have had an impact on my life and contributed to what I understand and believe. Without them, this book would not have been possible. There were many challenging times and, were it not for the support of my family and friends, I am not sure I would have been able to stay in this business for the past three decades.

First, I want thank my grandparents. All four of them came to this country from Italy/Sicily at the turn of the twentieth century and instilled in me my deep love for family and the art of caring for others. Even though they had not mastered the English language, they taught me the true meaning of communicating with IMPACT. The impact they had on me encouraged me to build deeper relationships with others and treat people like family. Thank you for taking the risk and pursuing the American Dream.

I want to thank my parents, Anthony and Filomena Donadio for instilling in me a good work ethic, faith, and creativity. From my dad, I learned about making others laugh, building relationships, and how to problem-solve. From my mother, I learned about unconditional love, caring for others before self, being a good listener, and how to cook. I would like to also thank my siblings, Rosemarie, Tony, Maria, and Jim, for their support, encouragement, and putting up with my weird sense of humor. As a middle child, I learned how to get attention, stand out from a crowd, and how to be a peacemaker. I especially want to thank my oldest sister "Roey." She was my number one fan. She laughed at all my jokes, encouraged me with countless thank you/love notes, and, in my younger years, put up with my using her as a practice guest for my many early talk shows we conducted at our kitchen table with my reel-to-reel tape recorder. Even though she is no longer with us, Roey's spirit lives on in me, encouraging me to help others.

To my wife, Beth, for all her support and encouragement. To my two children, Nicholas and Marissa, for all the joy they bring me and especially their understanding for what it takes to be an entrepreneur (the time I spent on the road and in the "black hole"—their name for my office).

They say, "It takes a village to raise a child," and that was true with me. I want to thank my hometown family and friends who were so instrumental in my early development. From my large Italian family to my Catholic upbringing and education, to my many teachers and mentors, to my neighbors and friends. So many people played a role in forming my personality and experience.

I especially want to thank:

All my aunts, uncles and cousins for their unconditional love and support. I was lucky to have so many of them around as I was growing up. Every Sunday at my grandparents' house, I had the opportunity to interact with older adults and cousins who helped me fine-tune my interpersonal communication skills.

Thank you to the priests, nuns, teachers and members of Our Lady of Mount Carmel Church and School. They played a pivotal role in my early spiritual development and helped me fine-tune my speaking and teaching skills. I spent many hours volunteering and helping at the church. Not only was I a reader at mass on Sundays, but I also taught C.C.D. (Confraternity of Christian Doctrine) classes to middle school students. I especially want to thank Pastor Fr. Nick Arioli for his guidance, Fr. Anthony Teolis for his drama and acting coaching, and Jane Cilletti, cook/spiritual adviser, for her love, wisdom and patience.

All my teachers and coaches at Niles McKinley High School. Especially principal Mr. Pallante, who allowed me to make the morning school announcements, which started me thinking about public speaking and radio/television work. Also, head football coach Anthony Napolet, who believed in me and encouraged me at a time when I didn't believe in myself.

To my many neighbors, especially the Sylvesters who lived next door as I was growing up, with whom I interacted and learned the value of friendship, fun, and giving.

To Ohio University professors, Administrators, co-workers, staff, and students. I chose to go to the Ohio University because I wanted to be a broadcaster and it was one of the best schools in the country for radio/television communication. I learned much more about communicating than just how to perform in front of a microphone and camera. Because of taking a job as a Resident Assistant to help pay for my college education, I learned about interpersonal communication as well. I moved up the ranks in Residence Life and, along the way, met some great mentors and staff.

Thanks to all my OU family for what they taught me about life and business.

Professional colleagues, coaches, and mentors including Kevin Buck, Tom Carlisi, and lifelong friend, Fr. Ron Nuzzi.

To my all National Speaker Association (NSA) friends and mentors who have helped me over the past twenty-five years that I have been a member. Without this group, I would not have had the courage, skill, or even motivation to write this book.

A special thank you to my NSA Ohio family who was there for me early in my speaking career when it was so unique to be a professional speaker and no one understood the challenges of the business like they did, especially Mike Frank, CSP, CPAE; Pat Vivo, CSP, CPAE; Charlie Dygert, CSP, CPAE; Patti Hathaway, CSP; Susan Schubert; Mike Kravitz; Carol Ritz, CSP; Barbra Braham, MCC; Barb Wingfield; Marie Pollack; Phil Sorentino, CSP; Jack Park, CPA, CSP; Angie Hollerich; Danielle Turcola; Richard Vail; Jim Canterucci; Lillian Zarzar, CSP; Rick Metzger, CSP; Kordell Norton, CSP; Rosemarie Rossetti, PhD; Fran Kick, CSP; Jon Petz, CSP; Kay Frances, MBA; and Randall Reeder.

I also want to thank all my NSA colleagues. NSA is an amazing association with giving members who have taught me so much about the speaking profession, and have encouraged and supported me along my journey: Nido Qubein, CSP, CPAE; Alan Weiss, CMC, CPAE, CSP, FCMC; Jim Cathcart Sr., CSP, CPAE; Glenna Salsbury, CSP, CPAE; Stephen C. Tweed, CSP, Elizabeth Jeffries, CSP, CPAE; Mark LeBlanc; Patricia Fripp, CSP, CPAE; Susan RoAne; Mark Sanborn, CSP, Robert H. Henry, CSP, CPAE; Ron Karr, CSP; CPAE; Ronald P. Culberson, MSW, CSP; Philip Van Hooser, CSP; Linda Byars Swindling, JD, CSP; Richard Avdoian, CSP, MS, MSW; Mark Hunter, CSP; Marcia Reynolds, CSP, MCC; David Meinz, CSP; James Rick; Jennifer Powers, MA; Wally Adamchik, CSP, CMC.

I know I might forget someone, so if I did and you are reading this, thank you!

Words cannot express my gratitude to my book coach, Kent Gustavson, PhD, for his professional advice, and his team at Blooming Twig for their assistance in polishing this manuscript.

A big thank you to all my speaking, training, and coaching clients who have hired me over the past three decades.

ABOUT THE AUTHOR

Patrick Donadio serves on the board of the National Speakers Association (NSA) and is one of only four people in the world to have earned both the Certified Speaking Professional (CSP) designation from the NSA, and the Master Certified Coach (MCC) designation from the International Coach Federation (ICF), the highest distinction from both associations.

Patrick has worked with thousands of leaders and their teams, from Fortune 100 companies to niche industries and associations, and he has been a national and international keynote speaker for thirty years. In his desire to help C-Suite executives and all leaders "grow their people" to greatness, Patrick has carefully taken his decades of experience and crafted a results-based process for Communicating with IMPACT, focused on improving communication, increasing profits, and boosting performance in less time.

After graduating Summa Cum Laude with a Bachelor's in Communications from The Ohio University, Patrick went on to receive his MBA in 1981. As an educator, he has taught communications at the University of Notre Dame, The Weatherhead School of Management, Ohio State University, and The John Glenn College of Public Affairs.

Patrick continues to speak, train, and coach across the country. He lives in Columbus, Ohio, with his wife, Beth, and has two grown children, Nicholas and Marissa.

Consider how Patrick Donadio can help you or your organization by having him speak at your next company meeting or association event. His high energy and highly interactive programs can be structured as a keynote or training for a full-day or half-day workshop.

To learn more about Patrick Donadio visit www.PatrickDonadio.com. You also can reach him at the below connections:

Phone: 614-488-9164
Email: Patrick@PatrickDonadio.com
LinkedIn: www.linkedin.com/in/patrickdonadio

HOW THE IMPACT PROCESS WAS BORN

The year was 1991, and I was in Japan as a goodwill ambassador for Rotary International on a group study exchange. Every few days, we stayed with a new host family and of course, each new family would do their best to give us their most gourmet dish for dinner.

Being of Italian decent, food is very important to me! If you ever visit any of my Italian-American relatives, they more than likely will want to feed you until the pasta comes out your ears. And if it is a special occasion, they will give you the best of what they have to offer.

So here I was in Japan, and these wonderfully hospitable families were serving their culinary best. I should have been thrilled. However, instead of serving what I was accustomed to (my family's succulent homemade ravioli, savory meatballs, and spicy wedding soup), they served various kinds of sushi.

As a kid, I enjoyed fish in several forms. Especially when it looked like the fish sticks my mother prepared on Fridays. Sushi was a far cry from the deep fried goodness of those fish sticks and, to say the least, I was not a fan!

If you were a sushi lover, you would have been in heaven at these host families' homes. The food at the first home, for example, was a veritable sushi smorgasbord, including unagi (eel), uni (sea urchin), tako (octopus), and ikura (salmon roe—ovaries or eggs). Unfortunately, the only kind of sushi that I could usually stomach was the "California roll" (an invention for the squeamish palates of Californians), which has crabmeat (or imitation crabmeat), avocado, and cucumbers (and no raw fish!), but they didn't have it.

Although not a fan of sushi, as a goodwill ambassador, I felt the need to be polite. Not to insult my host, I forced down various forms of the sushi set out in front of me. Luckily, they had some great cold biru (beer) to help me wash it down.

To my horror, my host slowly came towards me with a second full plate. I thought to myself, *Oh no, not a second plate!* Through my politeness, I had somehow inadvertently communicated that I love sushi.

My first host family communicated that I loved their sushi to the next two families. Now it was my third week in Japan and more sushi was coming. I was craving my comfort food. Anything besides raw fish would be great!

Luckily, my next host family had some younger children. With their help, we convinced their parents to take me to McDonald's.

When we walked into the McDonald's, I noticed they did have what I was craving: a Big-A-Macoo. That is what they call a Big Mac in Japan. It was almost six dollars, but I did not care. I would have paid $20. I wanted it!

So I ordered the Big-A-Macoo and fries.

As I was savoring my cooked American burger, I was thinking, *Oh, this is delicious!* It almost tastes like filet mignon.

Next, I tried the French fries and they were crunchy and salty—just the way I like them. I began to feel much better. My taste buds triggered in my brain the comfortable feeling of home.

While munching on the crispy potatoes that reminded me of America, I started thinking: *Isn't that amazing. I am halfway around the world and the French fries taste exactly the same.*

All of a sudden, it dawned on me. I felt at home in this Japanese McDonald's because the food tasted exactly the same as it did in Columbus, Ohio. In other words, anywhere you go in the world, you get McDonald's fries and they taste the same, because the McDonald's franchise wants your experience to be the same wherever you go.

Wow! I thought. *Wouldn't it be great if I had a proven process like that which would help me and my clients become better communicators?*

I was determined to turn my "franchise moment" into something meaningful.

Once back in the states, I continued to keeping thinking about the value of having a franchise-like communication system. Then it all came together when I read *The E-Myth* by Michael Gerber. This book reinforced the concepts for systematizing and franchising that I had encountered in the Japanese McDonald's. This realization changed the way I looked at my business.

I created the IMPACT process in this book largely based on the concept I first began to understand twenty-five years ago in that Japanese American restaurant.

Domo Arigato,

Patrick